AMAZING & EXTRAORDINARY FACTS

SHERLOCK HOLMES

AMAZING & EXTRAORDINARY FACTS

SHERLOCK HOLMES

NICHOLAS UTECHIN

David and Charles

CONTENTS

INTRODUCTION

There has not been a fictional character like Sherlock Holmes in the history of popular writing. Indeed, it is likely that a good proportion of those who have heard the name do not even know that he *is* a fictional character. I don't know how many times I have sat in a coach coming into London and, as the driver announces that his first stop will be in Baker Street, heard at least one person inform their companion that Sherlock Holmes used to live there. Tourists walk up and down the street every day, seeking out that famous address of 221B.

The very name of Sherlock Holmes has entered the English language. Whenever you come across the much-used phrase about the dog that didn't bark, you may not know that it derives from a Holmes story. Although he never actually said it in any of the stories, the phrase 'Elementary, my dear Watson!' is an immediate reference to the great consulting detective.

The deerstalker (invented for the character by one of his illustrators) and the curved pipe (brought to his lips by an actor) are immediately recognisable as *the* symbols for Holmes. He may have been created in the late 19th century, but the nine books containing his adventures have never been out of print. New generations of followers (called Holmesians in Britain and Sherlockians in the USA) are introduced all the time, not least because of the immense successes of the films starring Robert Downey Jr and Jude Law, and the reincarnation for the 21st century that is Benedict Cumberbatch and Martin Freeman as television's *Sherlock* and his friend John. Moreover, there are Sherlock Holmes societies all over the world.

Yet it was Arthur Conan Doyle who created and developed the characters of Holmes, Dr Watson, Mycroft Holmes, housekeeper Mrs Hudson and the 'Napoleon of Crime', Professor James Moriarty. It was Conan Doyle who invented two of the creepiest stories ever written: *The Hound of the Baskervilles* and 'The Adventure of the Speckled Band'. It was Conan Doyle who formed the partnership of Holmes and Watson that is at the heart of the long-standing success of the 56 short stories and the 4 longer ones.

It was also Conan Doyle who made his creations so believable – and the Victorian and Edwardian world in which they lived so real – that a whole form of pseudo-scholarship has grown up around them: a game, the writer Dorothy L. Sayers said in 1946, 'that must be played as seriously as a county cricket match at Lord's; the slightest touch of extravagance or burlesque ruins the atmosphere'. What this means is: forget that Sherlock Holmes is a fictional character and treat him as you would a real one. That means people can choose which university he attended, or how many wives Watson had or whether Holmes actually set out to murder Moriarty at the Reichenbach Falls in Switzerland.

Conan Doyle would have been amazed at the longevity of his characters: when he wanted to kill Holmes off, he wrote to his mother that 'he takes my mind from better things'. When the American actor William Gillette wanted to write a play based on the detective, he wrote to Conan Doyle asking if he might 'marry Holmes'. The author famously replied: 'You may marry him, murder him, or do anything you like to him.' Arguably, that gave the green light to all the pastiches that have placed Holmes with such people as Winston Churchill and Theodore Roosevelt, sent him off to Dallas to investigate Kennedy's assassination and to Whitechapel to confront Jack the Ripper.

No fictional character has so often been thrust on to the big screen than Sherlock Holmes. BBC radio has dramatised every single story, with the same two leading actors. The character has been used in advertisements from Fry's Cocoa to Air India, via Kalamazoo Gas Appliances and the New York Stock Exchange. There is a plaque commemorating the meeting of Holmes and Watson in Barts Hospital in London and a statue of the Great Detective outside Baker Street Underground Station. And it all started in Southsea, Hampshire, in 1886.

The Doyle family
Background of the author

Charles Altamont Doyle

A rthur Ignatius Conan Doyle was born at a house in Picardy Place, Edinburgh, on 22 May 1859. His birthplace was pulled down in later years, but a commemorative statue was unveiled in 1991, of Sherlock Holmes rather than Conan Doyle, a perfect example of how the created has triumphed over the creator.

His father was Charles Altamont Doyle; his mother was Mary Foley – she was to bear nine children. Although the author is universally referred to as Conan Doyle, Doyle was his actual surname, Conan being a family name. Doyle Senior worked from the age of 19 for the Scottish Office of Works as an architectural draughtsman, but was an alcoholic and an epileptic. It was one of the great tragedies of Arthur Conan Doyle's life that he had to commit his own father to an asylum. However despite the guilt he may have felt, he paid a form of tribute to his father years later when he gave Sherlock Holmes the pseudonym of 'Altamont' in the story 'His Last Bow'.

His mother, on the other hand, was to be a huge influence on Conan Doyle until the end of her life. 'My real love for letters,' Conan Doyle wrote, 'my instinct for storytelling, springs from my mother who is of Anglo–Celtic stock, with the glamour and romance of the Celt very strongly marked. In my early childhood, as far back as I can remember, the vivid stories she would tell me stand out so clearly that they obscure the real facts of my life.' Mary Doyle lived until 1920 and some 1,000 letters to her from her son exist.

ART IN THE BLOOD

The Doyles could draw. Conan Doyle's grandfather, John, was a leading political cartoonist, whose works appeared in **The Times** *from 1829 to 1851. His son Richard ('Dicky') drew for* **Punch** *and created the magazine's famous cover used from 1849 to 1956. Conan Doyle asked his father to provide a few illustrations for the first book edition of* **A Study in Scarlet** *– however they are not good.*

Stonyhurst College, Lancashire

Literary beginnings
Conan Doyle at school

It was necessary for Conan Doyle's mother to take in lodgers because of her husband's situation (see 'The Doyle family'), but money was available for her son's education. Conan Doyle was first sent to Hodder, an English Catholic preparatory school in Lancashire, and then on to Stonyhurst, a Jesuit foundation also in Lancashire.

He was to question the religious side of this education, but discovered that he could entrance his fellow students by telling stories: 'On a wet half-holiday I have been elevated on to a desk, and with an audience of little boys all squatting on the floor, with their chins upon their hands, I have talked myself husky over the misfortunes of my heroes.' During his time at Stonyhurst from 1868 to 1875, his favourite books were *The Water Witch* by Fennimore Cooper, *The Cloister and the Hearth* by Charles Reade and Sir Walter Scott's *Ivanhoe*.

It is likely that his schooldays influenced his later writings, and it is delightful to note that among those who arrived at the school with Conan Doyle was one Patrick Sherlock. Also at school with the author were two brothers from Ireland, Michael and John Moriarty; Michael was a fine mathematician whose surname and mathematical skill echo the character Professor James Moriarty in the stories. Furthermore, during the Christmas holidays in 1874, Conan Doyle was taken to see the waxwork show originally mounted by Madame Tussaud in London; it was not yet in Marylebone Road, but just around the corner, in Baker Street.

The Jesuitical side of his school education did not suit Conan Doyle and it is not difficult to see, in his eventual rejection of any form of organised religion, why he might be drawn as he was to the form of belief called Spiritualism.

Dr Joseph Bell
Mentor and model for Holmes

Twenty-two years older than Conan Doyle, Joseph Bell was, in 1876, a surgeon at Edinburgh Royal Infirmary and a professor at Edinburgh University. That was the year that Conan Doyle started to read medicine at the University and to attend Bell's classes. The following year Bell made the young student his outpatient clerk, which permitted him to watch the methods of the older man at close quarters.

A patient would come before Bell in one of the Infirmary's lecture theatres and, before an audience of his students, Bell would look the person up and down. On one occasion, Conan Doyle recalled, Bell explained how he had reached the conclusion that a patient had recently served as a non-commissioned officer in a Highland regiment in Barbados: '[T]he man was a respectful man but did not remove his hat. They do not in the army, but he would have learned civilian ways had he been long discharged. He had an air of authority and is obviously Scottish.

Joseph Bell

which I have seen you produce in the outpatient ward.' Indeed a year later Bell wrote an article entitled 'Mr Sherlock Holmes' for *The Bookman* which did not quite deny his own influence: 'Dr Conan Doyle's education as a student of medicine taught him how to observe, and his practice…has been a splendid training for a man such as he is, gifted with eyes, memory, and imagination… The experienced physician and the trained surgeon every day, in their examinations of the humblest patient, have to go through a similar process of reasoning, quick or slow according to the personal equations of each…'

Bell acted as Queen Victoria's personal surgeon whenever she was in Scotland, he edited the *Edinburgh Medical Journal* and is reputed to have been asked to help investigate the Jack the Ripper murders. His name lives on in Edinburgh University's Joseph Bell Centre for Forensic Statistics and Legal Reasoning, and he was portrayed by Ian Richardson in the BBC television series *Murder Rooms: The Dark Beginnings of Sherlock Holmes* (2000-01). It is inconceivable that Sherlock Holmes as we know

As to Barbados, his complaint is elephantiasis, which is West Indian and not British, and the Scottish regiments are at present in that particular land.'

In 1892, Conan Doyle dedicated the first book edition of *The Adventures of Sherlock Holmes* to Bell and wrote a letter to him that same year: 'It is most certainly to you that I owe Sherlock Holmes…I do not think that his analytical work is in the least an exaggeration of some effects him would have been created if Joseph Bell had never existed.

The doctor who wanted to write
Conan Doyle sets up practice in Southsea

A s a young doctor Conan Doyle set up practice in Southsea, near Portsmouth, in 1882. He says he made £154 in his first year, informing the Income Tax authorities that he was not liable. 'They returned the paper with "Most unsatisfactory" scrawled across it. I wrote "I entirely agree" under the words…'

Yet every now and then the doctor was augmenting his income by writing short stories, the format with which he was to eventually achieve his greatest success when he published his Sherlock Holmes short stories in *The Strand Magazine* (see '*The Strand Magazine*'). As early as 1879 his first work of fiction, 'The Mystery of Sasassa Valley', had been published in *Chambers's Journal* and long-defunct magazines such as *London Society, All The Year Round* and *Temple Bar* occasionally accepted other tales. In

Arthur Conan Doyle

1883 he began to write a novel, *The Narrative of John Smith*, which was so turgid that it remained unpublished until 2011.

Conan Doyle achieved some sort of a breakthrough the following year when the editor of the prestigious *Cornhill Magazine,* James Payn, accepted his short story 'J. Habakuk Jephson's Statement'. It was a gripping and clever account of how the *Marie Celeste* had famously been found abandoned without explanation. Here Conan Doyle provided an explanation, although no one knew that it was him, for the story was published – as was usual for the magazine – anonymously. It is a measure of the young doctor's story-telling powers that many readers thought it written by Robert Louis Stevenson. It also brought Conan Doyle a fee of £30.

Who came before?
Other literary detectives

In his autobiography, Conan Doyle only hints at Holmes' predecessors in fiction: 'Gaboriau had rather attracted me by the neat dovetailing of his plots, and Poe's masterful detective, M. Dupin, had from boyhood been one of my heroes. But could I bring an addition of my own?'

Commentators choose *Zadig* (1747) by Voltaire as the most important early example of detective work in fiction – this is essentially a philosophical novel, but powers of reasoning are on show as Zadig describes animals from the traces they have left behind. Then Eugène François Vidocq, a former criminal,

founded the Sûreté Nationale – a Scotland Yard equivalent – in France and published his memoirs in 1828. Vidocq operated as an individual private agent while running the Sûreté. He was much in favour of using disguises to help catch miscreants – as Sherlock Holmes did – and was the first investigator to make plaster-cast impressions of the imprints of shoes; Conan Doyle later had Holmes write a monograph on the subject.

However, as Conan Doyle pointed out, it was Edgar Allan Poe with his Chevalier Auguste Dupin who became the influential trailblazer, with the publication of his three stories 'The Murders in the Rue Morgue' (1841), 'The Mystery of Marie Roget' (1842) and 'The Purloined Letter' (1844). Conan Doyle will certainly have picked up on Dupin's words in 'Rue Morgue': '[I]t is in matters beyond the limits of mere rule that the skill of the analyst is evinced. He makes in silence a host of observations and inferences…'

Dorothy L. Sayers, in an essay on detective fiction published in 1930, explained the importance of what

Edgar Allen Poe

Poe did: '[T]he first thing that strikes us is that Poe has struck out at a blow the formal outline on which a large section of detective fiction has been built up. In the three Dupin stories, we have the formula of the eccentric and brilliant private detective whose doings are chronicled by an admiring and thick-headed friend…Poe stands at the parting of the ways for detective fiction. From him go the two great lines of development – the romantic and the classic…or…the purely sensational and the purely intellectual.' Sayers went on, in the same piece, to say: '[I]n 1887, *A Study in Scarlet* was flung like a bombshell into the field of detective fiction…'

Then, in 1868, came Sergeant Cuff in Wilkie Collins' *The Moonstone*, a book regarded by T. S. Eliot as 'the first, the longest, and the best of modern English detective novels' and by Sayers – later a leading contributor to Sherlock Holmes studies – as 'probably the very finest detective story ever written'. In the same year, Emile Gaboriau came up with the detective Monsieur Lecoq: 'In his hands,' writes the Conan Doyle biographer Andrew Lycett, 'the *roman policier* became a more cerebral, interactive medium.'

HOLMES HAS FUN

*There is no doubt that Conan Doyle distilled various elements of all literary predecessors in the creation of Sherlock Holmes, yet he had the nerve to disparage two of them straightaway in **A Study in Scarlet**. Here Watson says to Holmes: 'You remind me of Edgar Allan Poe's Dupin.' Sherlock Holmes lights his pipe: 'No doubt you think you are complimenting*

*me in comparing me to Dupin…
Now, in my opinion, Dupin was
a very inferior fellow. That trick of
his of breaking in on his friends'
thoughts with an apropos remark
after a quarter of an hour's silence
is really very showy and superficial.'
'Have you read Gaboriau's works?'
Watson asks. 'Does Lecoq come up
to your idea of a detective?' Holmes
responds: 'Lecoq was a miserable
bungler…he had only one thing to
recommend him, and that was his
energy. That book made me positively
ill…It might be made a text-book
for detectives to teach them what
to avoid.' In the light of Holmes'
dismissal of Dupin, five years later
readers of* **The Strand Magazine**
*with long memories will have enjoyed
this passage at the outset of 'The
Cardboard Box' story: 'Finding
that Holmes was too absorbed for
conversation I had tossed aside the
barren paper and, leaning back in
my chair, I fell into a brown study.
Suddenly my companion's voice broke
in upon my thoughts. "You are right,
Watson," said he, "It does seem a
most preposterous way of settling
a dispute." "Most preposterous!"*

*I exclaimed, and then suddenly
realizing how he had echoed the
inmost thought of my soul, I sat up
in my chair and stared at him in
blank amazement.'*

A Study in Scarlet
How Sherlock
Holmes was born

It is impossible to know now if
Conan Doyle's original names
for his detective and sidekick would
have taken on the same resonance
as 'Sherlock Holmes' and 'John H.
Watson'. It is surely unlikely, for a
page of scrawled notes on *A Study
in Scarlet* (at first to be called *A
Tangled Skein*) shows the writer's
first thoughts for these names to
have been 'Sherrinford Holmes' and,
unbelievably, 'Ormond Sacker'. In the
event, sanity prevailed.

In creating the character of
Holmes, Conan Doyle, in his
autobiography *Memories and
Adventures*, paid immediate tribute
to his Edinburgh mentor (see 'Dr
Joseph Bell'): 'I thought of my old
teacher Joe Bell, of his eagle face,

of his curious ways, of his eerie trick of spotting details. If he were a detective he would surely reduce this fascinating but unorganised business to something nearer to an exact science. I would try if I could get this effect. It was surely possible in real life, so why should I not make it plausible in fiction. It is all very well to say that a man is clever, but the reader wants to see examples of it – such examples as Bell gave us every day in the wards.'

An assistant for Holmes

Crucially, the concept of having an assistant for Holmes also came immediately: 'He could not tell his own exploits, so he must have a commonplace comrade as a foil – an educated man of action who could both join in the exploits and narrate them. A drab, quiet name for this unostentatious man. Watson would do. And so I had my puppets and wrote my "Study in Scarlet".'

It was not an entirely new literary concept in detective fiction, as we have seen with Poe (see 'Who came before?'), but Conan Doyle established it for the duration of the

60 stories, and it is perhaps the most famous and most copied one – Poirot has his Hastings, Morse his Lewis. The idea of having an associate present at and then narrating the cases is straightforward enough, but it is the juxtaposition of the brilliant and exciting Holmes with the 'everyman' of Watson that makes the device work so effectively. Indeed, the way that Watson conveys his own bafflement so well and often serves only to delight the reader.

Watson's medical and military background is quickly established in *A Study in Scarlet*, as he tells how he was invalided back to England after being wounded during the second Afghan War (this fact was instrumental to Stephen Moffat and Mark Gatiss kick-starting their television series *Sherlock* – why not a modern Watson, home from a 21st century conflict in Afghanistan?). Conan Doyle gave Dr Watson an exemplary prose style: '…I naturally gravitated to London, that great cesspool into which all the loungers and idlers of the Empire are irresistibly drained.'

'Dr Watson, Mr Sherlock Holmes.'

In London one day, with little to do, his pension running down and looking for somewhere to live, Watson bumps into Stamford – his former dresser at Barts Hospital – and wouldn't you know it? Stamford knows of someone who is also seeking to share quarters, and effects one of the most important introductions in popular literature: 'Dr Watson, Mr Sherlock Holmes.' Holmes' brilliance and Bell-like attributes are instantly established: 'How are you?…You have been in Afghanistan, I perceive.'

Weeks later, Holmes explained his thought processes: 'Here is a gentleman of a medical type, but with the air of a military man. Clearly an army doctor then. He has just come

Mormons crossing the plains of Nebraska

from the tropics, for his face is dark, and that is not the natural tint of his skin, for his wrists are fair. He has undergone hardship and sickness, as his haggard face says clearly. His left arm has been injured. He holds it in a stiff and unnatural manner. Where in the tropics could an English army doctor have seen so much hardship and got his arm wounded? Clearly in Afghanistan.'

The next day, the pair visit what has become one of the most instantly recognisable addresses in all fiction: 'We…inspected the rooms at No. 221B, Baker Street, of which he had spoken at our meeting. They consisted of a couple of comfortable bedrooms and a single large airy sitting-room, cheerfully furnished, and illuminated by two broad windows.' And there the two lived forever more – or at least until Watson left to get married for the first time and Holmes eventually retired to Sussex.

The story itself is not an amazing one and Conan Doyle is reliant on a very long section set in the USA: effectively – via a love story – retelling the tale of the Mormons and their trek to what became Salt Lake

City. Yet it is nevertheless the font from which the amazing Sherlock Holmes myth first grew.

WHERE DID *THOSE* NAMES COME FROM?

It is impossible to know for certain from where Conan Doyle selected the names of Holmes, Sherlock and Watson. In a speech he gave in 1921 he actually said 'I don't know how we got the name of Holmes'; however the origin can probably be straightforwardly identified as Oliver Wendell Holmes, the American doctor-philosopher. Conan Doyle once wrote 'Never have I so known and loved a man whom I have never seen' and, interestingly, Holmes spent three months in England during 1886 – the year A Study in Scarlet *was being written. Much has been made of cricket, a game that Conan Doyle played at a high level, in connection with the name of Sherlock: there was a county bowler named Frank Shacklock who played for Nottinghamshire and Derbyshire in*

the 1880s; and Mordecai Sherwin was the Nottinghamshire wicket keeper from 1878 to 1896. Conan Doyle could have mixed the two names together; however it is more likely that he recalled the Patrick Sherlock who had attended Stonyhurst (see 'Literary beginnings'). A cricketing connection can, however, almost certainly be made with Shacklock's partner in Derbyshire's fast bowling attack, William Mycroft: Mycroft was the name given to Sherlock's brother in the adventures. As we have seen, Conan Doyle wanted a 'drab, quiet name' for Holmes' room-mate and biographer, and there were a couple of Watsons to choose from: Dr Patrick Heron Watson had worked under Joseph Bell in Edinburgh and, closer to home, there was a Dr James Watson whose practice in Southsea was situated very near Conan Doyle's own. This Watson was also a member of the Portsmouth Literary and Scientific Society, whose meetings Conan Doyle enthusiastically attended.

A slow birth process
Beeton's Christmas Annual 1887

Conan Doyle started writing *A Study in Scarlet* on 8 March 1886, and he completed it barely a month later, sending it to James Payn at *The Cornhill Magazine* on 11 April. It was refused, as it was by two other publishers, Arrowsmith's and Frederick Warne, the latter later to bring Beatrix Potter to public acclamation. One cannot help comparing these decisions with those made by certain record executives in 1962 by their decisions not to sign The Beatles.

Conan Doyle was hurt. 'Finally,' he wrote, 'as Ward, Lock & Co. made a speciality of cheap and often sensational literature, I sent it to them.' Apparently the world must thank the wife of the company's editor-in-chief for persuading her husband that the story deserved publishing. Indeed the letter of acceptance sent to Conan Doyle on 30 October 1886 was hardly filled with praise: 'We have read your story and are pleased with it. We could not publish it this year as the market is flooded at present with

cheap fiction, but if you do not object to its being held over till next year, we will give you £25 for the copyright.' The young writer duly accepted the terms and payment. He never received another penny for *A Study in Scarlet*, although he was to make a fortune from his writings on Sherlock Holmes over the next 40 years.

The story eventually appeared in one of Ward, Lock's publications, *Beeton's Christmas Annual*, which hit the streets in late November 1887 and sold out before Christmas. It was the lead item in a one-shilling (5p) paperback, which also contained 'two original Drawing Room Plays' and 58 pages of advertisements. There were four illustrations by D. H. (David Henry) Friston who thus became the first in a long line of artists to portray Holmes. The writer of an article in *The Bookman* in 1932 was damning of Friston's work: 'This first picture of Holmes would distress the devotees. Friston's Holmes is neither handsome nor intellectual.'

This was the 28th such *Annual*, originally published under the editorship of Samuel Orchart Beeton, in a series which ran from

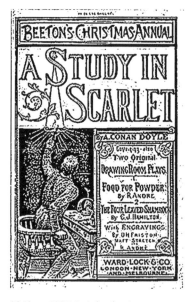

1860 to 1898. It is by far the most famous, although contemporary reviews of *A Study in Scarlet* were few and nothing special. Interestingly, Beeton had been married to Isabella Mary Beeton, compiler in 1861 of *Beeton's Book of Household Management* (yes, *that* Mrs Beeton).

INVALUABLE PAPERBACK

As the 1887 **Beeton's Christmas Annual** *contained the first appearance of Sherlock Holmes, it has become one of the most collectable magazines in the world. Only 32 copies are known to exist, in various states of condition. Twenty of them are held in libraries; no fewer than four of these at the University of Minnesota, USA. Currently, only six copies are known to be held in private hands. In 2007, a copy with a facsimile spine was sold at auction in New York for $156,000. In 2010, a copy with an inscription by Arthur Conan Doyle added on a separate sheet was withdrawn, unsold, at auction in London when bidding stopped at no less than £240,000. The Bodleian Library in Oxford has a copy with its covers and advertisements intact, but it is bound in hardback covers together with three other* **Annuals***. Perhaps the most interesting known extant copy consists of only the 95 pages of the* **A Study in Scarlet** *text, with none of the other contents, advertisements or covers; it does however carry these*

scribbled words on the first page:
'Return to Dr A. Conan Doyle.' – in
Conan Doyle's own hand. Why do
so few copies exist? Most **Beeton's**
Christmas Annuals *were read and*
then thrown away, as one might
discard a copy of a popular magazine
today. Yet anything is possible and
additional copies have been known
to appear: in the 1950s, a leading
British Holmes scholar found a
copy costing only a few shillings in
a London second-hand bookshop; a
bound copy turned up in an Oxfam
shop in 2008; and another such copy
in Australia in 2011.

Holmes described
Appearance, character
and background

On the day they first met in *A Study in Scarlet*, Holmes describes his own shortcomings to Watson: 'You don't mind the smell of strong tobacco, I hope?… I generally have chemicals about, and occasionally do experiments… Let me see, what are my other shortcomings? I get in the dumps at times, and don't open my mouth for days on end. You must not think I am sulky when I do that. Just let me alone, and I'll soon be right.'

The first physical description of Holmes appears a few pages later: 'In height, he was rather over six feet, and so excessively lean that he seemed to be considerably taller. His eyes were sharp and piercing, save during those intervals of torpor to which I have alluded; and his thin, hawk-like nose gave his whole expression an air of alertness and decision. His chin, too, had the prominence and squareness which mark the man of determination.' Elsewhere, Conan Doyle wrote: 'He had, as I imagined him, a thin razor-like face, with a great hawks-bill of a nose, and two small eyes, set close together on either side of it.' Holmes' hair is described as black, his lips thin, his brows dark and heavy, and his eyes grey. His voice was high and 'somewhat strident'.

In the story 'His Last Bow' – the final adventure, chronologically speaking – Sherlock Holmes, in disguise as the American agent Altamont, is described as being 'a tall, gaunt man of sixty'. Since the story is set at the outset of the First World War in 1914, it is generally accepted that Holmes was born in 1854. *A Study in Scarlet* took place in 1881, so Holmes was 27 when he and John Watson met; his brother, Mycroft, was seven years his senior. Holmes tells Watson that his ancestors were country squires 'who appear to have led much the same life as is natural to their class'. Yet, intriguingly, he reveals that his grandmother was the sister of 'Vernet, the French artist', a real person (Emile Jean Horace Vernet, 1789-1863). This immediately indicates that at least one of Holmes' squirearchical ancestors did *not* follow that natural path.

Holmes went to university – which one has been the subject of much discussion over the years – and it was while he was up at either Oxford or Cambridge that he first began to develop those skills that became his professional tools. We are not told exactly what he studied: the assumption by most scholars has been that it must have been chemistry, and certainly Holmes is reported in 'The Gloria Scott' to have done some experiments in organic chemistry

in the vacations. Arguments have also been put forward that he read Lit. Hum. (*Literae Humaniores*), which included the Greek and Latin languages and, crucially, Logic. When Watson first met him, Holmes was carrying out some research at Barts Hospital in London, although this was probably as the result of a short-term deal. 'His ignorance was as remarkable as his knowledge', Watson wrote of Holmes, and within a week he had even drawn up a list entitled 'SHERLOCK HOLMES – *his limits*'. It is a remarkable document:

'**1.** Knowledge of Literature – Nil.
2. Knowledge of Philosophy – Nil.
3. Knowledge of Astronomy – Nil.
4. Knowledge of Politics – Feeble.
5. Knowledge of Botany – Variable. Well up in belladonna, opium, and poisons generally. Knows nothing of practical gardening.
6. Knowledge of geology – Practical, but limited. Tells at a glance different soils from each other. After walks has shown me splashes upon his trousers, and told me by their colour and consistence in what part of

London he received them.

7. Knowledge of Chemistry – Profound.

8. Knowledge of Anatomy – Accurate, but unsystematic.

9. Knowledge of Sensational Literature – Immense. He appears to know every detail of every horror perpetrated in the century.

10. Plays the violin well.

11. Is an expert singlestick player, boxer, and swordsman.

12. Has a good practical knowledge of British law.'

In terms of character, Watson can be bleak about Holmes: '…the somewhat inhuman effect which he produced upon me…sometimes I found myself regarding him as an isolated phenomenon, a brain without a heart, as deficient in human sympathy as he was pre-eminent in intelligence' (from 'The Greek Interpreter'). And yet there were depths: in the story 'The Three Garridebs', Watson has just been shot and wounded: ' "You're not hurt, Watson? For God's sake, say that you are not hurt!" It was worth a wound – it was worth many wounds – to know the depth of loyalty and love which lay behind the cold mask. The clear, hard eyes were dimmed for a moment, and the firm lips were shaking. For the one and only time I caught a glimpse of a great heart as well as of a great brain.'

Watson described
Appearance, character and background

Internal evidence leads one to believe that Watson was born in 1852. At the close of the story 'Charles Augustus Milverton', which scholars have variously and unhelpfully dated between 1882 and 1889, he is described as 'a middle-sized, strongly built man – square jaw, thick neck, moustache'. Watson was probably quite handsome, since Holmes refers to his 'natural advantages' in relation to women.

There is absolutely no evidence provided of his family background – apart from the fact that he had a brother – but he was certainly sent to at least a minor public school since, in the adventure 'The Naval Treaty', the client is the nephew of a leading politician and a man with whom Watson had been at school and who went on to receive a scholarship to Cambridge. Watson is very detailed about his past in *A Study in Scarlet*, saying that he took a medical degree at the University of London (during which period

he somehow played rugby for the London club, Blackheath), then trained as an army surgeon at the medical hospital at Netley, near Southampton, and finally joined the Fifth Northumberland Fusiliers to go to war in Afghanistan, where he was wounded and nearly died.

We know that Watson visited Australia at one point in his life before meeting Holmes and he, intriguingly, boasted on one occasion of 'an experience of women which extends over many nations and three separate continents'. 'Now, Watson, the fair sex is your department,' said Holmes once, smiling knowingly. Watson married certainly once, probably twice and – because of internal chronological problems – at least one Holmes scholar has even suggested that Watson must have had five wives to make all the recorded facts fit.

In terms of his own shortcomings, Watson tells Holmes: 'I object to rows because my nerves are shaken, and I get up at all sorts of ungodly hours, and I am extremely lazy. I have another set of vices when I'm well', finishing on that bombshell.

Holmes' Baker Street
Numbers and complications

The Baker Street of today runs south from Park Road, adjacent to Regent's Park, to Portman Square, when it becomes Orchard Street shortly before its junction with Oxford Street. In the section north of Marylebone Road on the western side, the headquarters of the Abbey National Building Society occupied for many years the site that covered the famous 221B Baker Street address. Tourists these days should not be confused by the plaque attached to the adjacent Sherlock Holmes Museum announcing that it is 221B – those who run that commercial enterprise put this up. Yet when Holmes lived in 221B from, the scholars say, 1881 to 1903, neither of these buildings was even in Baker Street.

The original Baker Street was laid out during the 18th century by Edward Portman (1771-1823), named for a friend of the Portman family, Sir Edward Baker; it was the stretch that today runs down south from Crawford Street and Paddington Street to Portman Square. The part of

the street that runs from that junction north up to the Marylebone Road junction was known as York Place, and the northern extension beyond Marylebone Road was called Upper Baker Street. Interestingly, on the page of scribbled notes in preparation for *A Study in Scarlet*, Conan Doyle wrote the name 'Upper Baker Street'. It is, therefore, crucial that modern Holmesian researchers know this and understand that modern street numbers in the modern Baker Street bear no relation to the original street numbers. What is undoubtedly true is that Conan Doyle invented the 221B address in what was then Baker Street.

Years later, the writer claimed never to have visited Baker Street before choosing the thoroughfare as the home of Sherlock Holmes, but his memory had obviously failed him. Madame Tussaud originally set up her waxwork museum in Baker Street in 1835, and it remained there until outgrowing its site and moving to its present purpose-built structure around the corner in Marylebone Road in 1884. In an undated letter to his mother – but almost certainly from January 1874, when he was 15

years old – Conan Doyle wrote, while staying in London with his uncle, Dicky Doyle: 'I have been also to Madame Tussaud's, and was delighted with the room of Horrors, and the images of the murderers.' A very early and thought-provoking comment, one might suggest.

For many years during the 1950s and 1960s, there was on show in Madame Tussaud's present gallery a small-scale model 'diorama' of the pursuit of the Hound of the Baskervilles across Dartmoor; it remains in the archives, but inaccessible to the public. More recently, Robert Downey Jr was waxed up as Holmes when the first Guy Ritchie film was released in 2009; he certainly remains on view.

OTHER BITS OF BAKER STREET

During the Second World War, the Special Operations Executive (SOE) had its headquarters from 1940 at No. 64 Baker Street. The Beatles' Apple boutique occupied No. 94, at the eastern junction with Paddington Street, for one chaotic year (1967-68); and the singer Gerry Rafferty had an immense pop hit in 1978 with his song 'Baker Street' – there are, unfortunately, no Sherlock Holmes connotations in the lyrics. The Sherlock Holmes Hotel stands on the east side and, until a few years ago, there was a Dr Watson's Dental Practice in the same block.

So many choices
The search for 221B

Whenever the BBC presenter Terry Wogan used to cue in Gerry Rafferty's 'Baker Street' song, he invariably referred to it as one of the most boring streets in London. One has to agree: these days it is a fairly nondescript thoroughfare, with a mix of shops and restaurants similar to many others in the vicinity. However Sherlock Holmes lived there once, and we have an address to find.

It must immediately be pointed out that the 'B' in 221B was not part of the street number invented by Conan Doyle. It comes from the French term '*bis*', which merely indicates that Holmes and Watson lived in a subsidiary to the main street address – in this case on the 1st (US, 2nd) floor. That aside, it is only relevant to discuss *the* address in terms of the modern numbers.

The western side
The abode has to be on the western side of Baker Street, for very specific indications are given in the

1890   2010's

story 'The Empty House', when
Holmes and Watson are making
their way towards Baker Street to
catch Professor Moriarty's chief-
of-staff, Colonel Sebastian Moran.
A modern map of central London
will make perfect sense of what
follows: 'Holmes stopped the cab at
the corner of Cavendish Square…
Holmes' knowledge of the byways
of London was extraordinary…
We emerged at last into a small
road, lined with old, gloomy houses,
which led us into Manchester Street,

and so to Blandford Street. Here
he turned swiftly down a narrow
passage, passed through a wooden
gate into a deserted yard, and then
opened with a key the back door
of a house… "Do you know where
we are?" he whispered. "Surely
that is Baker Street," I answered…
"Exactly. We are in Camden House,
which stands opposite to our old
quarters." ' So they have approached
from the east and end up on the
eastern side of Baker Street.

No. 109

There have been many candidates for the original 221, and many years ago an American enthusiast made the staggering discovery that there was indeed a school named Camden House at No. 111 (on the eastern side) and thus No. 109 facing it was a brilliant candidate for the original 221. At the time of writing, 109 remains the only building in Baker Street with its ground floor frontage untouched, thus providing the true enthusiast with a feel for what the street as a whole might have looked like in Holmes' time. In terms of the Sherlock Holmes game, this was a wonderful discovery, but does not stand up because of one crucial passing remark made by Dr Watson at the start of the adventure 'Thor Bridge': 'It was a wild morning in October, and I observed as I was dressing how the last remaining leaves were being whirled from the solitary plane tree which graces the yard behind our house.'

No. 31

It is evident in black and white, in the 1895 Ordnance Survey map of Baker Street, that only No. 31 on the western side – three buildings south of the King Street and Blandford Street intersection with Baker Street – has a yard to its rear. And where did Watson say he and Holmes had ended up in that 'Empty House' trip on the eastern side of Baker Street? Blandford Street, and 'down a narrow passage'. Kendall Mews and other detailed topographical evidence means that they must have entered the back door of No. 34, diagonally opposite to No. 31. It is dangerous to be specific in such matters – and players of the game continue to have a lot of fun with the 221 identification – but No. 31 seems to be the best candidate. You can't see the original building today as the site has been enveloped by an immense modern construction, but No. 34 on the other side of the street – even though it too has been redeveloped – still at least looks the part.

THE IRREGULARS

Before leaving Baker Street, mention should be made of one of Conan Doyle's cleverest ideas when conceptualising the Sherlock Holmes stories: that of 'the Baker Street division of the detective police force'. With the best will in the world, Holmes could not by himself do all the research in every one of his cases; on occasion he needed help, and that was provided by a tight group of street urchins, led by a lad called Wiggins, who could 'go everywhere, see everything, overhear everything'. If the detective wants a specific hansom cab to be found, as he does in **A Study in Scarlet***, or a Thames steam launch, as he does in* **The Sign of Four***, he sends the Irregulars out to do the business. He pays them handsomely as well: a shilling (5p) a time, with a significant guinea (21 shilling) bonus to any boy who individually triumphs. The Baker Street Irregulars is the name taken by the most important Sherlock Holmes society in the USA, founded in the mid-1930s; their leader's title is always 'Wiggins'.*

The Sign of (the) Four
The story of the follow-up novel

In *A Study in Scarlet*, Conan Doyle had created two important characters and had provided them with a place to live. However, it is entirely possible that they might have languished relatively unknown in Baker Street forever after following that one adventure. At the time the author was actually hoping for success with novels such as *The Mystery of Cloomber* (1888) and the rather more exciting *Micah Clarke* a year later. Yet on 30 August 1889, an event took place in central London that revivified Holmes: a dinner party was held at The Langham Hotel.

Joseph Stoddart was a publisher by trade, who worked for an American company called J. Lippincott & Co. Publishing a monthly literary magazine in the USA called *Lippincott's*, they wanted to test the waters for an equivalent British version, so Stoddart came to London seeking authors. Here's the piece of fortune that led to a second tale starring Sherlock Holmes: the man

Stoddart wanted to edit this British *Lippincott's* was one George Bettany. It had been this man's wife who had spotted *A Study in Scarlet* three years earlier and had persuaded George to bring it out in the *Beeton's Christmas Annual* (see 'A slow birth process'). It is virtually certain that it was Bettany who suggested that Stoddart wine and dine Conan Doyle. Who suggested the other attendee is not known, but that second guest was

already rather better known than Conan Doyle: a certain playwright named Oscar Wilde.

Conan Doyle later referred to the event as 'a golden evening for me'. By the end of it, he had agreed – as he wrote in a diary entry for 30 August – 'to write story of 45,000 [words] for £100'. He wrote quickly: exactly one month later, his diary entry reads '*The Sign of the Four* finished and dispatched' and it was duly

The Langham hotel, London

published in the January 1890 edition of *Lippincott's* in the USA. There has always been a fuss about the title: the extra 'the' is present heading the front page of the story's manuscript – but it is not written in Conan Doyle's own hand. There was almost certainly a facing sheet, this time written by Conan Doyle, which had the title *without* that 'the'. You may take your pick, but the book's title today is generally accepted to be *The Sign of Four*. The literary result of that dinner so far as Wilde was concerned should also not be forgotten: it was *The Picture of Dorian Gray*.

The Sign of Four took the two main characters of Holmes and Watson into an exciting world of treasure, a chase down the Thames, some wonderful work with a dog and creosote, and also dropped the bombshell of Watson falling in love and becoming engaged. In addition, it also has the sort of ending that makes you feel you probably want to read more about these characters at some time in the future: ' "The division seems rather unfair," I remarked. "You have done all the work in this business. I get a wife out of it, Jones [the Scotland

Yarder] gets the credit; pray what remains for you?" "For me," said Sherlock Holmes, "there still remains the cocaine bottle." And he stretched his long, white hand up for it.'

THE LANGHAM
This famous hotel still stands in Portland Place, its outward appearance barely changed since its official opening by the Prince of Wales (later Edward VII) in June 1865. It was London's first 'purpose-built' grand hotel, costing £300,000 to build and incorporating 100 water closets, 36 bathrooms and the first hydraulic lifts in the country. Napoleon III, Mark Twain, Dvorak and Toscanini were among the guests over the years. For a time it was owned by the BBC – Broadcasting House stands on the other side of the road – and one famous radio announcer, sleeping in The Langham between shifts, swears he saw a ghost passing through his room. Whether this ghost was Conan Doyle, Oscar Wilde or, indeed, Sherlock Holmes, is not known. In 2010, a Westminster City Council green plaque was placed on the wall of The Langham,

outside the hotel's restaurant, to commemorate the famous literary dinner held in 1889 – it was unveiled by the writer, performer, broadcaster and former MP Gyles Brandreth.

Evocative of its time
Conan Doyle's London

Conan Doyle knew little of London until in 1891, aged 32, he moved from Southsea to lodgings near the British Museum to set up practice in the city as an oculist: 'I searched the doctors' quarters and at last found suitable accommodation at 2 Devonshire Place, which is at the top of Wimpole Street and close to the classical Harley Street. There for £120 a year I got the use of a front room and part use of a waiting room. I was soon to find that they were both waiting rooms.'

This is what he wrote in his autobiography but, bizarrely, Conan Doyle had actually forgotten the precise address in which he had sat waiting for patients. For years, it was accepted that 2 Devonshire Place had been his place of work;

indeed later the building was named Conan Doyle House, and so it remains today. Yet when, some years ago, the author's contemporary diary surfaced, the true address was revealed as having been 2 Upper Wimpole Street, a block further south. In 1994, a Westminster green plaque was mounted to the left of the property's doorway, commemorating the fact that Conan Doyle worked and wrote there in 1891.

In a sense, the actual venue makes little difference, for it was what did *not* happen at his office that is important. As Conan Doyle reminisced: 'Every morning I walked from the lodgings at Montague Place, reached my consulting-room at ten and sat there until three or four, with never a ring to disturb my serenity. Could better conditions for reflection and work be found? It was ideal, and so long as I was thoroughly unsuccessful in my professional venture there was every chance of improvement in my literary prospects. Therefore when I returned to the lodgings at teatime I bore my little sheaves with me, the first fruits of a considerable harvest.'

Harley Street, London

The word did not exist when Conan Doyle wrote his autobiography in 1924, but this is sheer 'spin'. You have here a far-from-raw medical practitioner arriving in London with a young family, making every effort to position himself perfectly for future advancement in his chosen profession – and not a single patient troubled him for several months. He must have been concerned, but then those 'little sheaves' were to prove vital to his future: his re-invention of Sherlock Holmes, in short story form.

He may not have known London well, but he certainly knew how to describe it. In *The Sign of Four*, he has Dr Watson write these atmospheric words: 'It was a September evening and not yet seven o'clock, but the day had been a dreary one, and a dense drizzly fog lay low upon the great city. Mud-coloured clouds drooped sadly over the muddy streets. Down The Strand, the lamps were but misty splotches of diffused light which threw a feeble circular glimmer upon the slimy pavement. The yellow glare from the shop windows streamed out into the steamy, vaporous air, and threw a murky shifting radiance across the crowded thoroughfare. There was, to my mind, something eerie and ghostlike in the endless procession of faces which flitted across these narrow bars of light – sad faces and glad, haggard and merry.' This is truly the London of Sherlock Holmes.

POPULATION PROBLEMS

What Conan Doyle wasn't very good at was being factually rigorous and consistent. He could be vague about dates, the position of Dr Watson's wound and even, on one unbelievable occasion, Watson's first name. London's population caused him some factual problems, too. In the short story 'The Blue Carbuncle', Holmes refers to 'one of those whimsical little incidents which will happen when you have four million human beings all jostling each other within the space of a few square miles'. In another story, 'The Cardboard Box', Watson describes the detective as loving 'to lie in the very centre of five millions of people, with his filaments stretching out and running through them'. Both cases

are dated to take place, most likely, in 1889; yet he presents a million difference in the population tallies. In reality the estimated population that year was some 4,352,000; but you can be sure Conan Doyle won't have known that.

The Strand Magazine
Reading for the masses

The Elementary Education Act of 1870, which provided for universal education of 5 to 12-year-olds, proved critical to the contemporary success of Sherlock Holmes. Until then, education in Britain had basically been a paid-for provision and was thus broadly available only to those who could afford it. Now, boards were set up to create schools in almost all urban and provincial areas and, some years later, Conan Doyle made Sherlock Holmes an enthusiastic supporter of the initiative.

In 'The Naval Treaty' (set in 1889 and published in 1893), Holmes and Watson are returning by train to London from Woking in Surrey:

educated class, and with the tentacles of cheap rail travel constantly extending, there became a need for journals and magazines to satisfy the newly educated young professional as he (yes, almost invariably a *he*) commuted to work. Pre-eminent among them was *The Strand Magazine*, whose first issue appeared in January 1891, priced at an accessible 6d. (2½p) a copy, which quickly attracted a readership of around 300,000. The magazine was paperbound, designed to be read over a journey or two and then (usually and tragically for later collectors) discarded.

Its publisher was George Newnes who, a decade earlier, had founded *Tit-Bits*, a magazine containing short extracts from other popular books and publications. *The Strand* announced that it would provide at least one picture on every page and would comprise a mix of fiction – often translations from the works of European writers – and factual articles. Each early issue contained approximately 100 pages of text and some 36 pages of advertisements, front and back. Its offices were located in London's Southampton Street,

'Look at those big, isolated clumps of buildings rising up above the slates, like brick islands in a grey-coloured sea,' says Holmes. Watson identifies them as the Board schools. Holmes' rejoinder is as follows: 'Lighthouses, my boy! Beacons of the future! Capsules, with hundreds of bright little seeds in each, out of which will spring the wiser, better England of the future.'

Popular writers like Conan Doyle benefited directly from this education initiative. With an expanding which runs north off The Strand, and Herbert Greenhough Smith edited it from the outset until 1930.

Sherlock Holmes revived

Conan Doyle and his literary agent, A. P. Watt, identified *The Strand* as a perfect vehicle for the plan the author had concocted: a revived Sherlock Holmes in short story form (habitually 7,500 to 8,500 words a piece), using the same basic Baker Street duo in each free-standing tale. On 30 March 1891, Watt received the first Holmes short story, 'A Scandal in Bohemia', from his client and sent it to Greenhough Smith, who immediately accepted it as the first of a series of six and offered to pay a rate of £4 per 1,000 words.

Conan Doyle was a speedy writer: on 11 April he delivered story number two, 'A Case of Identity' (not as good as the first) and, nine days later, 'The Red-Headed League' (one of the very finest). Those two were, incidentally, published in reverse order. 'A Scandal in Bohemia', running beneath the generic title 'The Adventures of Sherlock Holmes', appeared in the July issue,

publishing history was made, and Arthur Conan Doyle's life changed for ever more.

Sidney Paget
The first great Holmes illustrator

Several people had already illustrated Sherlock Holmes: D. H. Friston, Charles Doyle, George Hutchinson and James Greig provided art work for the early editions of *A Study in Scarlet*; the first appearances of *The Sign of Four* were without illustrations. However for the short stories that were to appear in *The Strand Magazine* (see '*The Strand Magazine*'), the publication's powers-that-be wanted to commission the best quality illustrations, especially since they were buying a series of tales, each of which would need to be accompanied by many pictures. So, they chose an experienced 28-year-old illustrator for the job named Paget – Walter Paget.

Apart from the fact that, as the story goes, they sent the offer by mistake to Walter's older brother, Sidney – who accepted the commission and produced more than 350 black-and-white illustrations for Holmes stories until his untimely death in 1908, aged just 48. Curiously, Walter did get to illustrate one Holmes adventure for the magazine – 'The Dying Detective', published in 1913 – but that was it.

Nevertheless Conan Doyle gave Walter his moment in the spotlight: '[A]ll the drawings are very unlike my original idea of the man…It chanced…that poor Sidney Paget who, before his premature death,

drew all the original pictures, had a younger brother whose name… was Walter, who served him as a model. The handsome Walter took the place of the more powerful but uglier Sherlock, and perhaps from the point of view of my lady readers it was as well.' Interestingly, this 'model allusion' is firmly denied in the 1912 Supplement to *The Dictionary of National Biography*. And so, Walter fades from the history of Holmes.

A significant contribution

In any event, Sidney created the look of Holmes and set the standard for years, at least for British readers. His output was phenomenal: ten illustrations for 'A Scandal in Bohemia', the same number for 'The Red-Headed League', seven for 'A Case of Identity' and so on. It isn't known if he was sent the full story texts, but he obviously required an idea of the plot outlines to decide which moments should best be highlighted. There was danger in this illustrative approach, of course: Paget's famous drawing of Holmes and Moriarty fighting above the raging Reichenbach Falls was published

Sidney Paget

as the first picture accompanying 'The Final Problem' – so readers would have known exactly what to expect in the story that followed. On the other hand, it was Paget we have to thank for gifting Holmes with one of his most essential, and durable, props. In only the fourth story, 'The Boscombe Valley Mystery', Conan Doyle gives him a 'close-fitting cloth cap' in which to travel to the country; in his illustrations, Paget made it a deerstalker.

It is a mark of how vital Conan Doyle knew Paget's contribution to be in the success of Holmes in *The Strand* that in 1893, on the occasion of Paget's wedding, he presented him with a silver cigarette case inscribed 'From Sherlock Holmes'. It is the only known object or book inscribed by the detective.

RARITY VALUE

Original Sidney Paget illustrations were available for purchase by the public after they had appeared in **The Strand Magazine,** *but today only 30 are known to exist, some most certainly destroyed by a fire at the magazine's offices. These pale wash drawings are now of great value. At a Sotheby's auction in London in July 1980, attended by this writer, three of the published illustrations were sold by one of Paget's sons. The cheapest auctioned for £950, the most expensive (probably because it came from* **The Hound of the Baskervilles***) for £2,500. How cheap those prices now seem: admittedly an iconic piece of work, in 2004 the original drawing of Holmes and Moriarty fighting at Reichenbach Falls was auctioned for $220,000.*

The human side
Re-introduction of Holmes

Actress Lillie Langtry, a
possible inspiration for Irene Adler

A s Conan Doyle introduced
Holmes to a new readership
at the launch of the series of short
stories published in *The Strand
Magazine*, he managed to achieve
something pretty extraordinary. In
the detective's first short story outing,
'A Scandal in Bohemia', the author
took several enormous risks. The very
first sentence of this story implies
a deep respect for a ('*the*') woman,
Irene Adler, a trained soprano and
regular adventuress. Then, in the
fourth and fifth sentences of the
story, as he is introducing Holmes
and Watson to a new audience, he
risks losing half of them at a stroke:
'It was not that he felt any emotion
akin to love for Irene Adler. All
emotions, and that one particularly,
were abhorrent to his cold, precise
but admirably balanced mind.'

This is in clear contrast to the
words with which Watson opens the
second paragraph, delivering a quite
extraordinary thumbnail sketch of
Sherlock Holmes: 'I had seen little
of Holmes lately. My marriage had

drifted us away from each other.
My own complete happiness, and
the home-centred interests which
rise up around the man who first
finds himself master of his own
establishment, were sufficient to
absorb all my attention; while
Holmes, who loathed every form of
society with his whole Bohemian
soul, remained in our lodgings in

Baker Street, buried among his old books, and alternating from week to week between cocaine and ambition, the drowsiness of the drug, and the fierce energy of his own keen nature.'

So, the reader is immediately told that Holmes could never love and is against emotions of any sort, that he is Bohemian, that he takes drugs and effectively has no friends. Does this present him as the ultimate anti-hero? Would you cross the road to shake the hand of Sherlock Holmes after this sort of introduction? On the other hand, perhaps such a man immediately intrigues you. The fact that Irene Adler actually *defeats* Holmes in this first story is again potentially literary suicide; but it clearly worked and, again, intrigued. This is brave, clever writing and yes, in the end, you do want to get to know this man.

Central attraction
Why Holmes still works today

The success of the original Canon of Sherlock Holmes stories – which means those written by Conan Doyle – is due to a feeling of familiarity: the fog, the hansom cabs rattling along the streets of London, the fire in the grate in the sitting-room of 221B Baker Street, the step of the client upon the stairs, the moments of action and lethargy, of Watson sitting down to read an exciting sea story by a favourite author, while Holmes scrapes discordantly on his Stradivarius violin or makes a series of extraordinary deductions from a walking stick.

We are drawn into the pleasure of the chase, the often seemingly irrational behaviour of Sherlock Holmes as he hurls himself to the ground as a sniffer dog might, his 'oohs' and 'ahs' as he places a hair in an envelope while Watson looks on *but does not observe*. We enjoy the constant bafflement of the Scotland Yard detectives, barring only Inspector Stanley Hopkins, and we finally revel in

the explanation at the end of the 8,000 words or so of a typical story.

Yet there is more. Yes, there are hansom cabs, but there are also cars. There are numerous telegrams, but there is, later on, a telephone. Conan Doyle kept the Baker Street duo moving with the times, while never losing the essentials. You may initially associate Sherlock Holmes with the autumn of the reign of Queen Victoria, until you recall that the last chronological case involving the detective takes place on the eve of the outbreak of the First World War. Indeed, the last story to appear was actually published in 1927.

The Sherlock Holmes stories are not simply page-turning whodunits in the style of an Agatha Christie thriller, where the only fun and interest lay in seeing who Poirot or Miss Marple would nail as the murderer. In a fair number of them, there is no actual crime committed. Yes, there are classics such as 'The Speckled Band' and 'The Bruce-Partington Plans' where there is indeed a killer to be tracked down. Yet for every one of those you have adventures like 'A Case of Identity' or 'The Yellow Face', into which Holmes is drawn merely by the quirkiness of events.

Deduction
It's a science

W ell, that's what Conan Doyle wrote in *A Study in Scarlet*, and it appears to be at the heart of what Sherlock Holmes did: he looks at someone, or something – as Dr Joseph Bell used to do – and decides who they are or what it is. Indeed, the examples are often at the core of the stories. 'You see but you do not observe,' Holmes tells Watson. Yet Holmes always observes, and he makes it clear how he reaches results in this way: 'By a man's finger nails, by his coat-sleeve, by his boot, by his trouser-knees, by the callosities of his forefinger and thumb, by his expression, by his shirt-cuffs – by each of these things

a man's calling is plainly revealed.'

He builds up a person's appearance and background from a walking stick in *The Hound of the Baskervilles* and a battered bowler hat in 'The Blue Carbuncle'. He counts how many miscreants have been present at a murder scene in 'The Abbey Grange' by looking at the residue in wine glasses. He sees cigar ash and knows how long a person has waited for a meeting. In his youth, he measured the length of a tree shadow and found a treasure. And it is during the adventure of 'Silver Blaze' that he tells the local policeman of the importance of the dog that did not bark.

In a less resounding fashion, Sherlock Holmes can tell Watson which side of a hansom cab he has chosen to sit in, to which street he went to transact business at a post office and what significance should be attached to the position of a light when he shaves. On one occasion Holmes joins forces with his brother Mycroft in a double act of detective expertise: they are standing at the window of Mycroft's club and looking down at a man in the street below. Watson records their ping-pong observations about him: ' "An old soldier, I perceive," said Sherlock. "And very recently discharged," remarked the brother. "Served in India, I see." "And a non-commissioned officer." "Royal Artillery, I fancy," said Sherlock. "And a widower." "But with a child." "Children, my dear boy, children." ' The explanations then follow, but the reader has been drawn in a long time ago.

A study of Watson

Watson himself is sometimes used by Holmes as a study for his methods, most spectacularly in that mind-reading sequence from 'The Cardboard Box'. The detective seems to be reading a letter while Watson is apparently doing nothing. After a time, Holmes utters two sentences: 'You are right, Watson…It does seem a most preposterous way of settling

a dispute.' In this order beforehand, Watson had looked at a portrait of General Gordon (of Khartoum), at a picture of Henry Ward Beecher and then at an empty space on the 221B wall. Within moments, the doctor had started thinking about what Beecher did during the American Civil War and, with his eyes sparkling and hands clenching, remembered the braveness shown by both sides in that conflict. Then he grew sadder, shook his head and touched his own war wound. Sherlock Holmes had followed all this and finally, seeing a wistful smile on Watson's lips, understood his companion's feeling of 'the ridiculous side of this method of settling international questions' – ie war – and interrupted Watson's reverie in the way he did. This is classic stuff, and Sherlock Holmes does it all the time.

The most moving example, perhaps, comes in *The Sign of Four* when Watson gives Holmes his pocket watch to look at to see if he can work out anything about its previous owner. 'He was a man of untidy habits – very untidy and careless. He was left with good prospects, but he threw away his chances, lived for some time in poverty with occasional short intervals of prosperity, and finally, taking to drink, he died. That is all I can gather.' Watson is deeply hurt, for the watch had been his brother's, and he accuses Holmes of already knowing about the brother's sad life. Sherlock Holmes retorts that he had not even known that Watson had a brother until he had passed the watch to him.

WHAT'S IT CALLED?

Not deduction. Throughout all the Sherlock Holmes stories he wrote, Conan Doyle got the word wrong: what Holmes did was in fact induction. Deductive reasoning works from the more general down to the more specific; inductive reasoning is the reverse. Thus in one story Holmes tells Watson that since he knows how he normally ties the laces on his boots, the fact that they have been 'fastened with an elaborate double bow' means that he must have attended a Turkish bath. From the specific – the double bow – to the general – the Turkish bath: this is induction.

Mycroft Holmes
Sherlock's big brother

Holmes' brother appears in only two of the stories and is mentioned in two others. Yet his formidable presence in 'The Greek Interpreter' and 'The Bruce-Partington Plans' made such an impact on audiences that he has become viewed as an integral part of the Baker Street ménage. Although he is nothing of the sort: 'Mycroft has his rails and he runs on them…His Pall Mall lodgings, the Diogenes Club, Whitehall – that is his cycle,' said Holmes. Thus his amazement when Mycroft announces his intention to come to 221B: 'It is as if you met a tram-car coming down a country lane…A planet might as well leave its orbit.'

Mycroft Holmes' job has nothing to do with detective work: he is a civil servant, but a most extraordinary one: 'You are right in thinking that he is under the British Government,' remarks Holmes to Watson, and then proceeds to give one of the many great quotations from the stories: 'You would also be right in a sense if you said that occasionally he *is* the British Government.'

That job of *being* the Government entails the use of his prodigious brain. Every decision made by government departments is passed to Mycroft and 'again and again his word has decided the national policy'. 'We will suppose,' Holmes explains to Watson, 'that a Minister needs information as to a point which involves the Navy, India, Canada and the bi-metallic question; he could get his separate advices from various departments upon each, but only Mycroft can focus them all, and say off-hand how each factor would affect the other.'

Watson's one-sentence description of Mycroft Holmes' physical appearance is as impressive a piece of writing as anywhere else in the 60 adventures: 'Heavily built and massive, there was a suggestion of uncouth physical inertia in the figure, but above this unwieldy frame there was perched a head so masterful in its brow, so alert in its steel-grey, deep-set eyes, so firm in its lips, and so subtle in its play of expression, that after the first glance one forgot the gross body and remembered

only the dominant mind.'

The Diogenes Club, incidentally, was a gentlemen's club – of which Mycroft Holmes was a founder – in which no member might speak to another save in the Stranger's Room. It was situated at the St James' end of Pall Mall.

MYCROFT STARS

The rôle of Holmes' brother has attracted actors of the highest quality – not all of who fitted Watson's physical description of the character. Robert Morley played Mycroft in the Jack-the-Ripper film **A Study in Terror** *(1965), and Derek Francis played him the same year on BBC television with Douglas Wilmer as*

Stephen Fry

Sherlock Holmes. Christopher Lee graced the Billy Wilder film **The Private Life of Sherlock Holmes** *(1970), then Charles Grey played the character on film in* **The Seven-Per-Cent Solution** *(1976) and on television a decade later in the Granada series with Jeremy Brett. Recently, Stephen Fry has played Mycroft in surprising (nude) fashion in* **Sherlock Holmes: A Game of Shadows** *and Mark Gatiss revels in the rôle in* **Sherlock** *on television.*

Mrs Hudson
The long-suffering landlady

When Holmes and Watson joined forces to rent the lodgings at 221B Baker Street, no mention was made of the landlady. Watson merely wrote that 'so moderate did the terms seem when divided between us, that the bargain was concluded upon the spot, and we at once entered into possession'. Those terms aren't known, but we do know from the outset in *A Study in Scarlet* that Mrs Hudson provided dinner as well as breakfast, that she

had a full-time maid working for her and that her tread was 'stately' as she went to bed at 11pm. How full-time the page boy Billy was is not known but, unlike the maid, he is not mentioned as having a bedroom. There is never even a passing mention of a Mr Hudson – alive or deceased.

By definition a landlady's role is generally peripheral, but then here her main tenant was unusual and – unintentionally – demanding. So we can understand her 'audible expressions of disgust' when the Baker Street Irregulars swarm upstairs in that first story. She is awoken well before 7.15 one morning to usher in Helen Stonor and the case of 'The Speckled Band', to lay a fire and stand ready to take an order for coffee. She will have been delighted that Sherlock Holmes chose to use a wall in the sitting room for target practice in 'The Musgrave Ritual', although the incident gave Watson an opportunity for one of his drier witty moments: 'I have always held… that pistol practice should distinctly be an open-air pastime; and when Holmes in one of his queer humours would sit in an arm-chair, with his

hair-trigger and a hundred Boxer
cartridges, and proceed to adorn
the opposite wall with a patriotic
V. R. done in bullet-pocks, I felt
strongly that neither the atmosphere
nor the appearance of our room was
improved by it.'

In 'The Mazarin Stone' Mrs
Hudson will doubtless have been
charmed, having asked Holmes when
he might like dinner, to receive the
classic reply 'Seven-thirty, the day

after tomorrow.' She will have been as
startled as Sherlock Holmes scholars
have been for years at the following
extract from 'A Scandal in Bohemia':
' "When Mrs Turner has brought in
the tray I will make it clear to you.
Now," he said, as he turned hungrily
on the simple fare that our landlady
had provided...' You can play the
game (Mrs Hudson had cooked the
food and her friend Mrs Turner had
brought it up to serve) or you can

put this down to an early piece of carelessness by Arthur Conan Doyle, that he completely forgot he had named the landlady 'Mrs Hudson' and inserted the random name of 'Mrs Turner' instead. This is in line with the occasion when Watson's own wife calls him James instead of John.

Returning to fiction, Mrs Hudson did much more than required of a landlady in 'The Empty House' when, under constant threat of gunfire, she regularly moved around a wax-bust placed in the 221B window to make it appear that it really was Sherlock Holmes. Moreover we know, from 'The Dying Detective', that she 'stood in the deepest awe of him'. Indeed, it is in this story that readers are given the truest picture of Mrs Hudson's views on Holmes: that she was long-suffering and must have had her patience tried by the detective, but that 'she was fond of him, too'. On the other hand, in a rare piece of cynicism, Watson reports in this same story that Holmes' payments for his rooms were by now 'princely'.

Scotland Yarders
Lestrade and all the rest

Apart from Dr Watson, Mycroft Holmes and Mrs Hudson, it is only the group of professionals from Scotland Yard who appear regularly in the stories, and by definition Holmes scores points over each of them and derides almost all. This treatment by Conan Doyle effectively set in stone the line to be taken by subsequent fictional private detectives. In the stories, 19 are mentioned by name, of whom Inspectors Lestrade, Hopkins and Gregson are the leading characters; others assisted by Sherlock Holmes included Inspectors Athelney Jones, Bradstreet, Macdonald, Gregory and Merivale.

Lestrade

Inspector George Lestrade appears right from the start in *A Study in Scarlet* and is featured in 12 further cases. Watson seems deeply unimpressed at the outset: 'There was one little, sallow, rat-faced, dark-eyed fellow, who was introduced to me as Mr Lestrade, and who came three or four times in a single week.' Not

Inspector Lestrade

only is he rude about the man's looks, but also he straightaway establishes his inadequacies as a detective, that he had to come running to Sherlock Holmes for help so often. Nevertheless, he and Tobias Gregson – who team up together in this first adventure – are described by Holmes as being 'the pick of a bad lot. They are both quick and energetic, but conventional – shockingly so.'

Lestrade is also described as being habitually out of his depth and lacking in imagination. On Dartmoor, at the point of crisis in *The Hound of the Baskervilles*, the professional 'gave a yell of terror and threw himself

face downwards upon the ground'. Yet he also displays 'bulldog tenacity' in one case and, at the close of 'The Six Napoleons' when Holmes has pulled off a revelatory triumph, nearly moves him to tears: 'We're not jealous of you at Scotland Yard. No, sir, we are damned proud of you, and if you come down tomorrow there's not a man, from the oldest inspector to the youngest constable, who wouldn't be glad to shake you by the hand.'

Gregson

Inspector Tobias Gregson is specifically described by Holmes in *A Study in Scarlet* as being 'the smartest of the Scotland Yarders', but early on is clearly not as generous as Lestrade turned out to be: 'He knows that I am his superior,' Holmes says, 'and acknowledges it to me; but he would cut his tongue out before he would own it to any third person.' At the time, Gregson and Lestrade were described as being direct rivals, presumably for promotion within the police organisation. Later however, in 'The Red Circle', Gregson joins the congratulatory bandwagon: 'I'll do you this justice,

Mr Holmes, that I was never in a case yet that I didn't feel stronger for having you on my side.' Watson responds in kind a moment later (a touch backhandedly), when the Scotland Yarder sets off to arrest a murderer: 'Our official detectives may blunder in the matter of intelligence, but never in that of courage.'

Hopkins

Of all the professionals, none is treated by Holmes with greater warmth than Inspector Stanley Hopkins. As Watson points out in 'The Golden Pince-Nez', Hopkins is 'a promising detective, in whose career Holmes had several times shown a very practical interest'. Indeed Hopkins had made an impression during the case of 'Black Peter': '[A]n exceedingly alert man, thirty years of age, dressed in a quiet tweed suit, but retaining the erect bearing of one who is accustomed to official uniform…a young police inspector for whose future Holmes had high hopes…'

THE YARD ITSELF

At the beginning of Holmes' career, London's Metropolitan Police force and the headquarters of its Detective Department – later to be named the Criminal Investigation Department – occupied premises in Great Scotland Yard, off Whitehall. The name stuck when the force was re-located in 1890 to its iconic building on the Victoria Embankment by the Thames – New Scotland Yard. It remained there for some 70 years until moving to even newer New Scotland Yard premises situated between Parliament Square and Victoria.

New Scotland Yard, Victoria Embankment

Professor Moriarty
The Napoleon of Crime

To paraphrase Sherlock Holmes: 'Is there any point to which you would draw my attention?' 'To the curious incident of Professor Moriarty'. 'Professor Moriarty never appears'. 'That was the curious incident.' Nowhere else in popular detective fiction is the leading criminal so absent. He is so famous, yet he appears in only three Holmes stories – and always at arm's length. Watson sees him once at a distance in Switzerland, but all other information about him comes second hand, from Holmes himself.

Professor James Moriarty was invented by Conan Doyle as a convenient gimmick of a character who could engineer Holmes' death. He therefore had to be a pretty special kind of criminal mastermind, an adversary worthy of Holmes, who describes him thus to Watson in 'The Final Problem': 'He is the organizer of half that is evil and of nearly all that is undetected in this great city. He is a genius, a philosopher, an abstract thinker. He

Paget's Professor Moriarty

has a brain of the first order. He sits motionless, like a spider in the centre of its web, but that web has a thousand radiations, and he knows well every quiver of each of them.'

Moriarty wrote a treatise on the Binomial Theorem when he was only 21 and was offered a Chair in

Mathematics 'at one of our smaller Universities', where he penned *The Dynamics of an Asteroid* – 'a book which ascends to such rarefied heights of pure mathematics that it is said that there was no man in the scientific press capable of criticising it'. After dark and unspecified rumours, he had to leave this post and came to London, setting up business as an army coach. However his earnings from crime were such that he could afford to buy a painting by the artist Jean Baptiste Greuze for £4,000, and to pay his chief-of-staff, Colonel Sebastian Moran, a staggering £6,000 a year.

After a game of cat-and-mouse stretching over several months, Holmes believed that he had at last organised a round up of the full Moriarty gang, but it was not to be and the stage was set for a final confrontation on a ledge above the Reichenbach Falls in Switzerland. Watson was sure that Holmes and Moriarty had perished during this encounter (see 'Reichenbach beckoned'). Eric Porter played Moriarty memorably in the Granada television series in 1985. More

recently, Jared Harris was a classically unpleasant Moriarty in *Sherlock Holmes: A Game of Shadows*, and Andrew Scott was utterly reptilian in his reinvention as Jim Moriarty in the BBC's *Sherlock*.

OTHER OPPONENTS

Moriarty was the greatest, and his chief-of-staff, Moran, was suitably dealt with by Holmes on his return from Reichenbach. Yet there were other fine baddies in the stories, some with fabulous names. One must be careful, for there are those who won't yet have read the Sherlock Holmes stories – but pay special attention to Grimesby Roylott in 'The Speckled Band' and Jephro Rucastle in 'The Copper Beeches'. Count Negretto Sylvius, from 'The Mazarin Stone', is an ungainly construction; the name Baron Adelbert Gruner from 'The Illustrious Client' has a pleasingly Middle-European dubiety about it; and the sheer crunch of the name Charles Augustus Milverton provides a frisson (in the eponymous story) that would be rendered utterly harmless if you took either the 'Charles' or the 'Augustus' away.

Women and Holmes
What he really thought of them

Gayle Hunnicutt, who played Irene Adler in The Adventures of Sherlock Holmes, *1984*

This is a complicated area. So much has been written and implied about Sherlock Holmes and his lack of interest in women – and therefore allegations of being gay that ask to be refuted – that one may only examine the various relevant quotations and use them to reach a sensible conclusion.

Thus in the first short story 'A Scandal in Bohemia' – in which Irene Adler will always be to Holmes '*the* woman' because she defeated him – readers must travel a few lines down from the top of the tale to learn that 'He never spoke of the softer passions without a gibe and a sneer.' Early on in *The Sign of Four,* Watson points out that their client Mary Morstan (later to be his wife) is 'a very attractive woman!' Sherlock Holmes drooped his eyelids and replies: 'Is she?…I did not observe.' Watson immediately accuses him of being inhuman, to which the still-languid Holmes replies, in part, that 'the most winning woman I ever knew was hanged for

poisoning three little children for their insurance-money'. Later in the same story, he comes out with the fairly brutal judgement that 'Women are never to be entirely trusted, not the best of them.' In 'The Second Stain', he maintains that 'the motives of women are so inscrutable'. Thus he is, on the basis of professional experience, not too keen on them.

However there are several balancing examples recorded by Watson. At the culmination of 'The Devil's Foot', Holmes speaks (almost) emotionally:

'I have never loved, Watson, but if I did and if the woman I loved had met such an end…' So the possibility of love is certainly not ruled out. There is an interesting passage as the story of 'The Copper Beeches' opens, when the client, a young lady named Violet Hunter, arrives in Baker Street: 'I could see that Holmes was favourably impressed by the manner and speech of his new client. He looked her over in his searching fashion…' Moments later, in the only example of flirtatiousness involving Holmes recorded by Watson, Miss Hunter says: 'As you may observe, Mr Holmes, my hair is somewhat luxuriant, and of a rather peculiar tint of chestnut. It has been considered artistic.' Sherlock Holmes does not react directly, but at the very close of the story, when all has been satisfactorily resolved, Watson says intriguingly: 'As to Miss Violet Hunter, my friend Holmes, rather to my disappointment, manifested no further interest in her…' He cannot have written those words if he knew that Holmes was truly uninterested in the opposite sex.

There is also a very important passage in one of the later stories,

'The Lion's Mane', written by Holmes himself after retiring to Sussex. He meets a young woman called Maud Bellamy, and his flowery description of her gives the lie to any implications – frequently made in the modern era – that Holmes was gay. I quote it in full: 'There is no gainsaying that she would have graced any assembly in the world. Who could have imagined that so rare a flower would grow from such a root and in such an atmosphere? Women have seldom been an attraction for me, for my brain has always governed my heart, but I could not look upon her perfect clear-cut face, with all the soft freshness of the Downlands in her delicate colouring, without realizing that no young man would cross her path unscathed.' Holmes' brain is not working all that hard at this point.

It must be said that Sherlock Holmes behaved extremely badly and dishonourably with a woman in the adventure called 'Charles Augustus Milverton'. It is not giving too much away to say that Milverton was a blackmailer and an arch-swine, and Holmes needed to know the layout of his house in Hampstead. So what does he do? He takes up with Milverton's housemaid, Agatha, and becomes engaged. Watson is not happy, but Holmes airily announces that 'I have got all I wanted…I rejoice to say that I have a hated rival…' However disgraceful the behaviour, there is here absolute proof that – even though it was done for a practical purpose – Sherlock Holmes knew how to chat up a woman, successfully.

Holmes' literary tastes
What he reads and what he recommends

William Winwood Reade

Sherlock Holmes is rather annoying when referring to his favourite authors: he has a blasé approach more redolent of Highgate literary soirées than Baker Street bohemianism. Moreover he is a show-off, which must surely have been tedious for Watson, who enjoyed nothing more than immersing himself in an exciting tale of naval derring-do by the popular writer William Clark Russell. 'Are you well up in your Jean Paul?' Holmes demands of Watson, who at least knows who is being referred to and responds

valiantly: 'Fairly so. I worked back to him through Carlyle.' Holmes is remorseless in his one-upmanship: 'That was like following the brook to the parent lake.' Jean Paul, incidentally, was the popular name for Johann Paul Friedrich Richter, a German writer (1763-1825) of romances with philosophical overtones.

In *The Sign of Four*, Holmes utters an interesting throwaway line to Watson: 'I am going out now. I have some few references to make. Let me recommend this book – one of the most remarkable ever penned. It is Winwood Reade's *Martyrdom of Man*. I shall be back in an hour.' Luckily at this point Watson is thinking too much of the attractions of their client, Mary Morstan, to respond, but the subject of the book – a history of the Western world from a secular viewpoint, published in 1872 – says much about Holmes', and Conan Doyle's, near-atheism. At the very end of this adventure, Holmes blithely quotes from Goethe.

In a far more surprising example of his literary tastes, Holmes interrupts discussion of the ins and outs of 'The Boscombe Valley Mystery' by saying to Watson: 'And now here is my pocket Petrarch, and not another word shall I say of this case until we are on the scene of action.' The real mystery here – unresolved, for the poet is never mentioned again – is why Sherlock Holmes thought so much of the lyric poems written in the 14th century by Francesco Petrarch, dealing with infatuated love for his muse, that he carried a book of them around with him. Hidden depths indeed.

Otherwise, Holmes regularly quotes from Shakespeare, knows his Balzac and his Thoreau, his Keats and his Longfellow. Conan Doyle will have assumed that his *Strand* readers – accustomed in that publication to seeing translations of stories by Guy de Maupassant and the like – would very likely recognise all the authors he introduced to Holmes' world.

Holmes' musical tastes
The detective takes time to relax

Watson was made aware of Holmes' musicality at their first meeting. While the two were making sure that they could share lodgings together, Watson mentioned that he objected to rows. 'Do you include violin playing in your category of rows?' Holmes asks, anxiously. Watson replies that he has no objection if the instrument is well played, and his query is thus brushed away by Holmes.

Which is not surprising since Holmes owned a very great instrument, as Watson reports during a break in the action of the adventure 'The Cardboard Box': '… Holmes would talk about nothing but violins, narrating with great exultation how he had purchased his own Stradivarius, which was worth at least five hundred guineas, at a Jew broker's in Tottenham Court Road for fifty-five shillings. This led him to Paganini, and we sat for an hour over a bottle of claret while he told me anecdote after anecdote of that extraordinary man.'

An appreciation, and knowledge, of music runs through the stories: Watson describes Sherlock Holmes as

Nicolo Paganini

'not only a very capable performer, but a composer of no ordinary merit'. Any true lover of classical music will recognise this lyrical description of Holmes as he attended a concert in the St James's Hall in the story 'The Red-Headed League': 'All the afternoon he sat in the stalls wrapped in the most perfect happiness, gently waving his long thin fingers in time to the music, while his gently smiling face and his languid dreamy eyes were as unlike those of Holmes the sleuth-hound…as it was possible to conceive.' Unsurprising, perhaps, since the duo was hearing the greatest of contemporary violinists, Sarasate. At the close of 'The Red Circle', Holmes hurries Watson off to a Wagner night at Covent Garden. Furthermore, the operatic singing brothers, the de Reszkes, are mentioned in *The Hound of the Baskervilles* as performing in Mayerbeer's 'Les Huguenots'; Holmes has a box to see them.

During *A Study in Scarlet*, one of the most aggravating of all musical references in the stories is made by Holmes as he prepares for a concert with one of the great violinists: 'And now for lunch and then for

Norman-Neruda. Her attack and her bowing are splendid. What's that little thing of Chopin's she plays so magnificently: "Tra-la-la-lira-lira-lay?" ' For Holmesian scholars of a musical persuasion, trying to identify this scrap has provided years of entertainment. One of the leaders in the field, Guy Warrack, a fine musician and conductor himself, plays the game excellently in *Sherlock Holmes and Music,* 1947: 'Watson's musical notation makes it difficult to identify the "little thing" conclusively. On *prima facie* evidence we might incline towards the Nocturne No. 15 in F minor, although if this presumption is correct Watson has omitted one "la"…'

SHERLOCK'S MUSICIANSHIP

It is one of the elements in portraying Holmes on the small or large screen that must be the most demanding and annoying for actors; for it is accepted that, just as he wears a deerstalker, smokes a curved pipe and waves a magnifying glass around, so there has always to be the odd moment of Holmesian rumination with a violin within a production. Yet very few of the major actors can play the instrument. So it has become a spectator sport to enjoy the obvious sound dubbing and approximate fingering: much easier to 'scrape carelessly at the fiddle which was thrown across his knee', as described in **A Study in Scarlet.** *However within Sherlock Holmes film orchestration, a wonderful piece of violin composing, or adaptation, was done by Miklos Rosza for* **The Private Life of Sherlock Holmes** *(1970), and by Patrick Gowers for the 1980s and 1990s Granada television series.*

A rare actor
Sherlock Holmes in disguise

Holmes loved dressing up, something that was obviously very necessary in his profession. Yet it was clearly not merely a matter of putting on makeup and different clothing: 'You would have made an actor and a rare one,' Inspector Athelney Jones told him. Watson was very astute: 'He had at least five small refuges in different parts of London, in which he was able to change his personality' and, even more perceptively: '[H]is very soul seemed to vary with every fresh part that he assumed.'

Holmes had a fondness for the cloth, disguising himself as an aged Italian priest as he and Watson tried to evade recognition by Moriarty or his agents in 'The Final Problem', and as an 'amiable and simple-minded' Nonconformist clergyman in 'A Scandal in Bohemia'. In fact, that was the second disguise he had donned in that story: he had earlier researched Irene Adler's St John's Wood surroundings in the disguise of a drunken-looking groom. Watson sums up the brilliance of what Holmes was able to achieve in that 'Final Problem' episode: 'The aged ecclesiastic had turned his face towards me. For an instant the wrinkles were smoothed away, the nose drew away from the chin, the lower lip ceased to protrude and the mouth to mumble, the dull eyes regained their fire, the drooping figure expanded.' Not a mention is made here of any makeup.

Holmes' most successful disguise must, in a sense, have been the one he adopted when wooing Charles Augustus Milverton's housemaid. Appearing as 'a rakish young workman with a goatee and a swagger' – he told Agatha he was a plumber with an increasingly successful business – he must have come quite close physically to the poor girl on a number of occasions for them actually to have become engaged, yet avoided detection. Furthermore, in 'The Mazarin Stone' he dresses up as a woman, the only example of this extreme form of disguise in the stories, although Holmes does say to Watson, 'You've seen me as an old lady', so he must have done it at least once previously.

In his final case, 'His Last Bow', Holmes, at the age of 58, took on his greatest disguise: that of someone else entirely for two years as he assumed the identity of a Chicago crook, Altamont, in his pursuit of German agents as the First World War loomed.

It is perhaps one of the most predictable moments in any Sherlock Holmes film that the detective turns up in a disguise: it is bound to happen. The most outrageous examples in recent years occur (twice) with Robert Downey Jr in *Sherlock Holmes: A Game of Shadows*.

Town versus country
Holmes, the city-dweller

One of the great attractions of the Sherlock Holmes stories lies in their sense of place, and that place is London. We have already seen how Conan Doyle adapted his own lack of first-hand knowledge of the capital to produce a good literary sense of place once he himself began living there (see 'Evocative of its time'). Yet as the stories developed, the author added layer upon layer of detail to Holmes' love of the city – and built up in his

character a serious case of loathing for the countryside.

'He loved to lie in the very centre of five millions of people,' wrote Watson, establishing the point immediately in 'The Cardboard Box'. Moreover Holmes seems to visit the world of J. M. Barrie's *Peter Pan* in another story, 'A Case of Identity', specifically in praise of living in London: 'If we could fly out of that window hand in hand, hover over this great city, gently remove the roofs, and peep in at the queer things which are going on, the strange coincidences, the plannings, the cross-purposes, the wonderful chains of events, working through generations, and leading to the most outré results, it would make all fiction with its conventionalities and foreseen conclusions most stale and unprofitable.'

Watson can provide a passing architectural reference with resonance: 'Caulfield Gardens was one of those lines of flat-faced, pillared and porticoed houses which are so prominent a product of the middle Victorian epoch in the West-end of London.' He can

Vauxhall Bridge, London

also allow Holmes to deliver a geography lesson that an owner of the *London A-Z* would be proud of, as they are driven to an unknown destination in *The Sign of Four*:

'…I lost my bearings, and knew nothing, save that we seemed to be going a very long way. Sherlock Holmes was never at fault, however, and he muttered the names as the cab rattled through squares and in and out of tortuous by-streets. "Rochester Row," said he. "Now Vincent Square. Now we come out on the Vauxhall Bridge Road. We are making for the Surrey side, apparently. Yes, I thought so. Now we are on the bridge. You can catch glimpses of the river." We did indeed get a fleeting view of a stretch of the Thames, with the lamps shining upon the broad, silent water; but our cab dashed on, and was soon involved in a labyrinth of streets upon the other side. "Wordsworth Road," said my companion. "Priory Road. Lark Hall Lane. Stockwell Place. Robert Street. Cold Harbour Lane. Our quest does not appear to take us to very fashionable regions."'

'The Copper Beeches'

Holmes' abhorrence of the countryside has its most obvious expression in the story 'The Copper Beeches'. Holmes and Watson are on a train travelling to Winchester; Watson's light and very English descriptions of the views from the carriage are in perfect counterpoint to Holmes' crushing rejoinders:

'It was an ideal spring day, a light blue sky, flecked with little fleecy white clouds drifting across from west to east. The sun was shining very brightly, and yet there was an exhilarating nip in the air, which set an edge to a man's energy. All over the countryside, away to the rolling hills around Aldershot, the little red and grey roofs of the farm-steadings peeped out from amidst the light green of the new foliage. "Are they not fresh and beautiful?" I cried, with all the enthusiasm of a man fresh from the fogs of Baker Street. But Holmes shook his head gravely. "Do you know, Watson," said he, "that it is one of the curses of a mind with a turn like mine that I must look at everything with reference to my own special subject. You look at

these scattered houses, and you are impressed by their beauty. I look at them, and the only thought which comes to me is a feeling of their isolation, and of the impunity with which crime may be committed there." "Good heavens!" I cried. "Who would associate crime with these dear old homesteads?" "They always fill me with a certain horror. It is my belief, Watson, founded upon my experience, that the lowest and vilest alleys in London do not present a more dreadful record of sin than does the smiling countryside." '

The latter sentence is the famous part of the quotation, yet Holmes continues with an interesting justification for his views:

'The reason is very obvious. The pressure of public opinion can do in the town what the law cannot accomplish. There is no lane so vile that the scream of a tortured child, or the thud of a drunkard's blow, does not beget sympathy and indignation among the neighbours, and then the whole machinery of justice is ever so close that a word of complaint can set it going, and there is but a step between the crime and the dock. But look at these lonely houses, each in its own fields, filled for the most part with poor ignorant folk who know little of the law. Think of the deeds of hellish cruelty, the hidden wickedness which may go on, year in, year out, in such places, and none the wiser. Had this lady who appeals to us for help gone to live in Winchester, I should never have had a fear for her. It is the five miles of country which makes the danger.'

Holmes argues that his dislike of the countryside is based on criminal factors and is surprisingly rude about 'poor, ignorant' country folk, but it is fairly clear that he would not be a natural dweller anywhere much beyond London's boundaries. Yet, intriguingly, when he retired, he chose to move to a remote cottage on the Sussex Downs.

Expert monographs
Holmes, the writer

It was in the very first story, *A Study in Scarlet*, that Holmes revealed himself to be an author when, in only one of the three examples we know of, he has an article published in a journal. Unfortunately we don't know which journal this was, since Watson refers to it only as a 'magazine'. The article's title was 'The Book of Life' and it essentially laid down the Joseph Bell-like practicalities of observation: 'From a drop of water, a logician could infer the possibility of an Atlantic or a Niagara without having seen or heard of one or the other. So all life is a great chain, the nature of which is known whenever we are shown a single link of it.'

Watson was actually annoyed when he read it: 'What ineffable twaddle!…I never read such rubbish in my life.' Sherlock Holmes then reveals that he is the author and uses the opportunity to explain to the doctor – after several weeks' of acquaintanceship in sharing 221B Baker Street – what he actually does for a living: 'I suppose I am the only one in the world. I'm a consulting detective…Here in London we have lots of Government detectives and lots of private ones. When these fellows are at fault, they come to me, and I manage to put them on the right scent.'

So far as the two other publicly published articles are concerned, Sherlock Holmes mentions them in the case of 'The Cardboard Box', saying that he had published two 'monographs' in the previous year's *Anthropological Journal,* almost certainly the *Journal of the Anthropological Institute of Great Britain and Ireland.* This particular case concerned severed ears, and the specialist papers in question demonstrated that each ear differs from every other one.

Gradually, as the adventures proceed, we gather that Holmes has in fact penned quite a number of specialist monographs. The most famous was *Upon the Distinction Between the Ashes of Various Tobaccos* in which he listed 140 forms of cigar, cigarette and pipe tobacco, and all their differing forms of ash. His descriptive words are redolent of an age when Conan Doyle's readers

would have been far more aware of smoking than they would be today: 'If you can say definitely, for example, that some murder had been done by a man who was smoking an Indian lunkah, it obviously narrows your field of search. To the trained eye there is as much difference between the black ash of a Trichinopoly and the white fluff of bird's-eye as there is between a cabbage and a potato.' In fact, Conan Doyle wrote that he had once been asked by a tobacconist in Philadelphia for a copy of the brochure.

In a similar vein, Holmes wrote a 'trifling' monograph analysing 160 separate ciphers and publications on the dating of documents, the tracing of footsteps, and tattoos. He was especially proud of his 'curious little work upon the influence of a trade upon the form of the hand, with lythotypes of the hands of slaters, sailors, cork-cutters, compositors, weavers, and diamond-polishers'. He displayed his knowledge in this field on first meeting Violet Smith, 'The Solitary Cyclist', holding her hand and saying: 'You will excuse me, I am sure. It is

Orlandus Lassus

my business…I nearly fell into the error of supposing that you were typewriting. Of course, it is obvious that it is music. You observe the spatulate finger end, Watson, which is common to both professions?'

In an altogether different area of endeavour – and born out of what was a hobby rather than his job – Holmes spent a day during the progress of the case called 'The Bruce-Partington Plans' working on a monograph on the Polyphonic Motets (more than 500 of them) by the 16th century composer Orlandus Lassus. Watson reports that it was later 'printed for private circulation, and,' – wouldn't you

believe it – 'is said by experts to be the last word on the subject'.

Finally, during his retirement keeping bees in Sussex, he produced what he described as his magnum opus, the *Practical Handbook of Bee Culture, with some Observations upon the Segregation of the Queen*. Whether or not he ever completed his *Whole Art of Detection* is not known. Somewhat surprisingly, not a single copy of any of these priceless pieces has ever been discovered – or at least come to the marketplace.

ANOTHER PUBLISHING MYSTERY

When **A Study in Scarlet** *first appeared in* **Beeton's Christmas Annual** *for 1887, Conan Doyle had the nerve to start playing a game that did not yet exist; the tale appeared as 'Being a reprint from the reminiscences of John H. Watson MD, late of the Army Medical Department.' So the hare was set running, posing the question: where is the original from which the reprint was taken? This is a question Sherlock Holmes scholars have never been able to answer.*

Great quotations
Holmes, the brilliant conversationalist

Sherlock Holmes was a brilliant conversationalist, excellent at delivering aphorisms and superbly obscure in some of the deductions he made and the roundabout ways in which he occasionally delivered them. Indeed, it will have been a sheer delight for Watson to record over the years such quotes as these:

➤ 'Mediocrity knows nothing higher than itself, but talent instantly recognises genius.'

➤ 'When you have eliminated the impossible, whatever remains, however improbable, must be the truth.'

➤ 'It is a capital mistake to theorise before one has data. Insensibly one begins to twist facts to suit theories, instead of theories to suit facts.'

➤ 'It is quite a three pipe problem, and I beg that you won't speak to me for fifty minutes.'

➤ 'You know my method. It is founded upon the observation of trifles.'

➤ 'Now, Watson, the fair sex is your department.'

➤ ' "I followed you." "I saw no-one." "That is what you may expect to see when I follow you." '

➤ 'You mentioned your name as if I should recognise it, but beyond the obvious facts that you are a bachelor, a solicitor, a Freemason and an asthmatic, I know nothing whatever about you.'

➤ 'Come, Watson, come! The game is afoot! Into your clothes and come!'

➤ 'The Press, Watson, is a valuable institution, if you know how to use it.'

➤ 'My professional charges are upon a fixed scale. I do not vary them, save when I remit them altogether.'

➤ 'Come at once if convenient. If inconvenient – come all the same.'

➤ 'I never guess. It is a shocking habit – destructive to the logical faculty.'

Most contemplative of all

'Our highest assurance of the goodness of Providence seems to me to rest in the flowers. All other things, our powers, our desires, our food, are really necessary for our existence in the first instance. But this rose is an extra. Its smell and its colour are an embellishment of life, not a condition of it.'

Most emotional of all

On the eve of the outbreak of the First World War: 'There's an east wind coming…such a wind as never blew on England yet. It will be cold and bitter, Watson, and a good many of us may wither before its blast. But it's God's own wind none the less, and a cleaner, better, stronger land will lie in the sunshine when the storm has cleared.'

And, most classic of all

' "Is there any other point to which you would wish to draw my attention?" "To the curious incident of the dog in the night-time." "The dog did nothing in the night-time." "That was the curious incident," remarked Sherlock Holmes.'

WHAT HE DID NOT SAY

Sherlock Holmes never uttered the words 'Elementary, my dear Watson' in the stories. 'Elementary', yes; 'My dear Watson', several times – but never together. Yet it has become the single most famous aphorism associated with Holmes. It is alleged – but there is no proof – that the American actor William Gillette used it on stage in his play **Sherlock Holmes** *(1899); it is not in the script. However P. G. Wodehouse, a lover of Conan Doyle's works, did use the phrase in his book* **Psmith, Journalist** *(1915). And in the 1929 film* **The Return of Sherlock Holmes,** *Clive Brook as Holmes says: 'Elementary, my dear Watson, elementary.'*

The early plots
Short story breakdown, Part 1

Conan Doyle's imagination, and audacity, in his plot lines for the first 24 stories that made up *The Adventures* and *The Memoirs* is worth recording. That said, no plots will be spoiled in this listing. The following are short précis of my own:

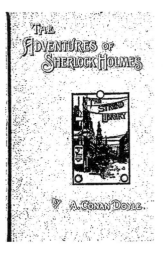

A SCANDAL IN BOHEMIA: European royalty, blackmail, female adversary, no crime.

A CASE OF IDENTITY: Disguise, greed, stupid female client, petty middle-class tale, no crime.

THE RED-HEADED LEAGUE: Red herrings abound, bewildered male client, clever adversary, robbery envisaged.

THE BOSCOMBE VALLEY MYSTERY: The first murder in the short stories, country location, historical background to crime.

THE FIVE ORANGE PIPS: Unlucky client, genuine brain teaser, more than one murder, historical background.

THE MAN WITH THE TWISTED LIP: Red herring territory initially, mix of London characters, frightened female client, superb and surprising plot resolution.

THE BLUE CARBUNCLE: One of the best pieces of 'hat' detective work in fiction, off-beat goose puzzle, seasonal Christmas feel, two sad characters, theft.

THE SPECKLED BAND: Frightened female client, worst villain in all the stories, murder, atmosphere abounds, as do animals.

THE ENGINEER'S THUMB: Great story title, perplexing plot, scientific knowledge a bonus, home counties location, background crime that could lead to something worse.

THE NOBLE BACHELOR: Class attitudes abound, male-female entanglements, historical background, Scotland Yard bafflement, no crime.

THE BERYL CORONET: Aristocratic class involvement, panicky banker client, jewel-encrusted poser, family problem, no real crime.

THE COPPER BEECHES: Classic female client of quality, puzzling story involving hair and laughter, unpleasant adversary with tawdry designs, no crime.

SILVER BLAZE: Best quotation in all the stories, genuine mystery in country horsey circles, death, excellent whodunit.

THE CARDBOARD BOX: Most tragic case in all the stories, fine characterisations, murder, seething passions, deeply atmospheric.

THE YELLOW FACE: Seemingly intriguing at first, meandering later, historical background, no crime, Conan Doyle at his first loose end.

THE STOCKBROKER'S CLERK: Midlands-based, business chicanery, genuinely puzzling plot, near-death, various crimes.

THE 'GLORIA SCOTT': Complete change of pace – tale from the past recounted by Holmes to Watson, historical backgrounds all round, more than one villain, important in the Oxford-Cambridge controversy.

THE MUSGRAVE RITUAL: Second story in a row to be told by Holmes as a throw back to early days, historical background, mathematical puzzle, no direct adversary but a death in fraught circumstances, important in the Oxford-Cambridge controversy.

THE REIGATE SQUIRES: Home counties action, murder, attempted murder, Holmes on his toes throughout.

THE CROOKED MAN: Family tragedy, passion, death, historical background.

THE RESIDENT PATIENT: Standard mystery, strange foreigners, useless client, murder.

THE GREEK INTERPRETER: More foreigners, clever mystery, much Mycroft (good!), murder and near murder.

THE NAVAL TREATY: Classic, a rare real whodunit, classic quotes from Holmes, everything in place.

THE FINAL PROBLEM: Professor Moriarty, Reichenbach Falls, Holmes' death, Watson's despair, beyond classic.

Holmes is critical
Watson's writing analysed

'The Copper Beeches' was published in the June 1892 edition of *The Strand Magazine* as the 12th and last of *The Adventures of Sherlock Holmes* and is fascinating for one reason. Not the plot – although it is a very serviceable one, involving a governess who is obliged by her employer to have a very specific sort of luxuriant hair and always to sit at the same time of day in a very specific place – but for the way that the story is opened by Sherlock Holmes.

He and Watson are in Baker Street, and the detective is bored. So, most surprisingly, he criticises the doctor's style of writing up his cases, becoming more and more critical: '[T]hese little records of our cases which you have been good enough to draw up, and, I am bound to say, occasionally to embellish'; 'You have erred, perhaps, in attempting to put colour and life into each of your statements, instead of confining yourself to the task of placing upon record that severe reasoning from cause to effect which is really the only notable feature about the thing'; 'You have degraded what should have been a course of lectures into a series of tales'; '[I]n avoiding the sensational, I fear that you may have bordered on the trivial.'

This was Conan Doyle being audacious in the extreme, almost turning against his own enormous success with the characters and tales by having the 'hero' figure (Holmes) castigate his biographer. It may have been an in-joke, or perhaps a deliberate ploy to show off a new Holmesian characteristic by building a tension between him and Watson. Or perhaps it was something more sinister, betraying in a clever way the very first stirrings of dissatisfaction with this popular success ('bordered on the trivial') that led Conan Doyle, 18 months later, to kill off his great creation.

CURIOUS STORIES NOT TOLD BY WATSON

Whatever the reason for including Holmes' critique of Watson's writing style (see 'Holmes is critical'), Conan Doyle played the game more light-heartedly years later, long after he had resuscitated Holmes. Indeed he had Holmes write one of his own stories, 'The Blanched Soldier', which was published in November 1926: '…I am compelled to admit that, having taken my pen in my hand, I do begin to realize that the matter must be presented in such a way as may interest the reader.' Conan Doyle was either very pleased with the result, or lazy, or could not care, for the very next story, 'The Lion's Mane', was also presented as written by Holmes. Two other stories, 'The Mazarin Stone' and 'His Last Bow', appear as having been written in the third person. In any case, they must all have appeared very strange to readers of The Strand Magazine, *lulled over the decades into familiarity with the Watson format.*

Increasing returns
Conan Doyle and his considerable earnings

Arthur Conan Doyle was no businessman – as some rather stupid investments he made in later years proved – but he soon realised the intrinsic worth of the Sherlock Holmes stories to *The Strand Magazine* and others, and was helped by his astute choice of literary agent, A. P. Watt, to realise the stories' financial potential. He never forgot that he had naively sold the entire copyright of *A Study in Scarlet* in 1886 for the sum of just £25. For his subsequent novel, *The Sign of Four*, he received from *Lippincott's* publishers £100 in 1889; his initial deal with *The Strand* for the short stories that followed was £4 per 1,000 words.

'A Scandal in Bohemia' came in at approximately 8,500 words, thus entailing a payment of £34, although the magazine was so pleased with their new star that this figure was rounded up to £36. Payment for each of the first six adventures – up to the wonderfully-titled 'The Man with the Twisted Lip' – averaged £35. In the

meantime, his agent Watt had sold US publishing rights of those initial six stories to a newspaper syndicate for a total of £50.

Naturally *The Strand* wanted more stories, so Conan Doyle asked for more money – at his request for £50 per story, this equated to some 40 per cent more. The magazine did not balk at the price for a second. Interestingly this impelled the author to write better stories: 'I was determined, now that I had no longer the excuse of absolute pecuniary pressure, never again to write anything which was not as good as I could possibly make it, and therefore I would not write a Holmes story without a worthy plot and without a problem which interested my own mind, for that is the first requisite before you can interest anyone else.'

And this all happened again. At the beginning of 1892, *The Strand* wanted a further set of 12 stories, to start publishing at the end of the year. This series was eventually to be called *The Memoirs of Sherlock Holmes*. Conan Doyle and Watt asked for £1,000 for the 12. Again, the magazine did not demur and 'Silver Blaze' duly appeared in the December issue.

In context

It would be useful to put these sums of money into a modern context. Using the retail price index comparing purchasing powers, one indicator (www.measuringworth. com) shows that you would have needed to pay £84.80 in the year 2010 for what £1 would buy in 1892: in short a ratio of 85 to 1. On that basis we can see, in today's values, the increase in price per Sherlock Holmes story that Conan Doyle achieved in just one calendar year (the figures are not precise, but close enough):

January 1891 (first six *Adventures*): £2,975 (£35 x 85)
July 1891 (second six *Adventures*): £4,250 (£50 x 85)
January 1892 (the 12 *Memoirs*): £7,055 (£83 x 85)

To put it another way, Conan Doyle was paid for the first 24 Sherlock Holmes short stories, working at the ratio of 85 to 1, a total of £128,010. This was a very solid set of pay cheques. He was also beginning to receive invitations to speak to audiences (18 guineas, for example, for a talk on the author George Meredith – around £1,600 today). Another indicator, incidentally, makes the value of the 1892 £1 closer to £100 now – which would make Conan Doyle even luckier.

His fortune was made – and of course, he was writing other fiction, too. Indeed the Conan Doyle biographer, Andrew Lycett, notes from the writer's personal notebooks that he earned £2,729 in the year 1892 (writing a total of 214,000 words), which equates to around £230,000 in today's money by the yardstick we are using.

Reichenbach beckoned
The killing of Sherlock Holmes

In early 1893, Conan Doyle decided to kill his golden goose, for what he thought were reasons of quality: 'I saw that I was in danger of having my hand forced, and of being entirely identified with what I regarded as a lower stratum of literary achievement. Therefore as a sign of my resolution I determined to end the life of my hero.'

On 6 April, he wrote to his mother from his London home: 'All is very well down here. I am in the middle of the last Holmes story, after which the gentleman vanishes, never never to reappear.' At that moment, he had still not determined how exactly to carry out the deed, but a trip to Europe with his wife helped: 'The idea was in my mind when I went…for a short holiday in Switzerland, in the course of which we saw there the wonderful falls of Reichenbach, a terrible place, and one that I thought would make a worthy tomb for poor Sherlock, even if I buried my banking account along with him.'

Paget's death fight at Reichenbach Falls

'It is with a heavy heart that I take up my pen to write these the last words in which I shall ever record the singular gifts by which my friend Mr Sherlock Holmes was distinguished.' This was the opening line of 'The Final Problem' that faced dumbstruck *Strand* readers in the December issue of the magazine. These words were accompanied with the famous opening illustration by Sidney Paget of the death

fight at Reichenbach between Holmes and Professor Moriarty.

In his peroration, Conan Doyle had Watson write some valedictory words: 'An examination by experts leaves little doubt that a personal contest between the two men ended, as it could hardly fail to end in such a situation, in their reeling over, locked in each other's arms…[T]here, deep down in that dreadful cauldron of swirling water and seething foam, will lie for all time the most dangerous criminal and the foremost champion of the law of their generation.'

There is absolutely no doubt that Conan Doyle was bored with Sherlock Holmes by this time and genuinely wished to write about other things – even if that 'banking account' was going to be emptier than heretofore. However hindsight is everything, and one wonders if those precise words 'as it could hardly fail to end' were precisely placed to provide the author with the tiniest of options for the future.

In the short term, the reaction was extraordinary, and in his autobiography Conan Doyle told the story: '[T]he general protest against my summary execution of Holmes taught me how many and how numerous were his friends. "You Brute" was the beginning of the letter of remonstrance which one lady sent me, and I expect she spoke for others besides herself. I heard of many who wept.' Indeed there are famous, perhaps apocryphal, stories at the time of young businessmen in the City wearing black armbands.

Sherlock Holmes memorial at Meiringen, Switzerland

THE FAMOUS REICHENBACH FALLS

The Falls had been famous before Conan Doyle buried (or not) Holmes at their base: J. M. W. Turner had painted them twice, in 1802 and 1804. They are near the village of Meiringen in the Swiss canton of Bern, where there is a seated statue of Sherlock Holmes, as well as a museum. Holmes groups have placed commemorative plaques in the vicinity of the Falls, and the Sherlock Holmes Society of London has made much-publicised costumed visits to them – the first in 1968 – which always culminate in two dummies being hurled into the 'dreadful cauldron'. For the 1985 Granada television film of the story, two stuntmen made the jump for real in front of the cameras.

Start of something
The Holmes phenomenon

The public reaction to Conan Doyle's killing of Holmes was intriguing. It was nothing new for readers to grieve: tears had been shed years earlier, for example, when Charles Dickens allowed Little Dorrit to die. Yet, while Conan Doyle perfectly understood that his creation had been a money-spinner for him, he did not at this moment realise exactly what he had achieved. It was, for many, as if a real life had been snuffed out, so cleverly engineered had been the Baker Street milieu. Conan Doyle had written the tales so quickly and so easily that he did not comprehend the substance of what he had invented.

An article about him, 'A Day with Dr Conan Doyle', had appeared in *The Strand* of August 1892, written by the magazine's reporter-at-large, Harry How. At the time, enthusiasm for Sherlock Holmes was already apparent and the magazine's editor, Greenhough Smith, undoubtedly wished to boost it further. How described the writer's approach to his Holmes stories: 'Dr Doyle invariably conceives the end of his story first, and writes up to it. He gets the climax, and his art lies in the ingenious way in which he conceals it from his readers. A story – similar to those which have appeared in these pages – occupies about a week in writing, and the ideas have come at all manner of times – when out walking, cricketing, tricycling, or playing tennis. He works between the hours of breakfast and lunch, and again in the evening from five to eight, writing some three thousand words a day.'

However, it was the opening lines of this article by Harry How that were the most interesting. Again written for *Strand* publicity reasons, it is one of the first examples of an attempt to explain the Holmes phenomenon – decades before societies and journals started to be devoted to it: 'Detectivism up to date – that is what Dr Conan Doyle has given us. We were fast becoming weary of the representative of the old school; he was, at his best, a very ordinary mortal, and, with the palpable clues placed in his path, the average individual could easily have cornered the "wanted" one without calling in the police or the private inquiry agent. Sherlock Holmes entered the criminal arena. He started on the track. A clever fellow; a cool, calculating fellow, this Holmes. He would see the clue to a murder in a ball of worsted and certain conviction in a saucer of milk. The little things we regarded as nothings were all and everything to Holmes. He was an artful fellow, too; and though he knew "all about it" from the first, he ingeniously contrived to hold his secret to the very last line in the story. There never was a man who propounded a criminal conundrum and gave us so many guesses until we "gave it up" as Sherlock Holmes.'

Allowing for a certain degree of exaggeration and a touch of tautology, How pinpointed the appeal accurately. Yet neither he nor

Arthur Conan Doyle's house, South Norwood

his interviewee could possibly have guessed at that point just how strong a hold Holmes would eventually have on the public's imagination, in both Britain and around the world.

First parodies
Sherlock Holmes becomes a copied man

On 9 April 1892, four months before the Harry How piece (see 'Start of something'), something unusual appeared in a penny magazine, *The Ludgate Weekly*. It was entitled 'Adventures of Sherwood Hoakes – Adventure 1: The Interrupted Honeymoon', apparently written by A. Cone and Oil, and is the first known parody of a Sherlock Holmes short story. The author's real name was C. C. Rothwell.

Of greater and more lasting literary importance was the next such parody, published in one of *The Strand Magazines's* popular competitors. *The Idler Magazine – An Illustrated Monthly* (its full title) had first appeared in February 1892 and was edited by a Canadian writer, Robert Barr, and Jerome K. Jerome. Like *The Strand*,

Jerome K. Jerome

The Idler went in for short stories, humour, light-hearted political commentary and memoirs: indeed Conan Doyle had his own short story, 'De Profundis', published in its second issue.

However in May 1892, a story appeared called 'Detective Stories Gone Wrong – The Adventures of Sherlaw Kombs'. It was written by Luke Sharp (Barr's pseudonym) and, bracketed beneath the rather lumbering title, were the words:

'(with apologies to Dr Conan Doyle, and his excellent book, *A Study in Scarlet*)'. Ten months after 'A Scandal in Bohemia' came out, the first important Sherlock Holmes parody had been penned – recognition in a very public way of the success of the original. It is a light, whimsical bit of fun, with a witty opening, by Whatson [sic]:

'I dropped in on my friend Sherlaw Kombs, to hear what he had to say about the Pegram mystery, as it had come to be called in the newspapers. I found him playing the violin with a look of sweet peace and serenity on his face, which I never noticed on the countenances of those within hearing distance. I knew this expression of seraphic calm indicated that Kombs had been deeply annoyed about something. Such, indeed, proved to be the case, for one of the morning papers had contained an article eulogising the alertness and general competence of Scotland Yard. So great was Sherlaw Kombs's contempt for Scotland Yard that he never would visit Scotland during his vacations, nor would he ever admit

that a Scotchman was fit for anything but export.' It hardly comes as any surprise that Kombs fails to solve the case correctly.

Thus began a passion for parody over the years, with the name of Sherlock Holmes transmuted in extraordinary ways, from Picklock Holes and Padlock Jones, via Herlock Sholmes and Shamrock Wolmbs, to Porlock Moans and Townclock Fumes. And so, of course, there have had to be a Squatson, Whatsup and Potsdam, among many others.

THE IDLERS

The Idler Magazine *survived until 1911, a year before its editor, Robert Barr, died, who Conan Doyle had described as having 'a violent manner, a wealth of strong adjectives, and one of the kindest natures underneath it all'. The magazine attracted writers of high calibre, including Hall Caine, Max Beerbohm, Rider Haggard and Rudyard Kipling; a book by Mark Twain,* **The American Claimant,** *was serialised over the magazine's first six issues. One of its regular contributing illustrators* *was George Hutchinson, who had drawn the pictures for the second book edition of* **A Study in Scarlet.** *There was a social side to those who contributed, with Conan Doyle – a keen sportsman – at the heart of it. In a letter dated 16 August 1892, he wrote thus: 'My dear Barr – Jerome will tell you how keen I am about an Idlers Match on September 7th (Wednesday). Mind that you come, for if you don't play cricket you play base ball [sic] and can field & we'll all just do our best…' For the record, the match was duly played – against Conan Doyle's local club in Norwood, London. Barr did turn out for the Idlers, as did E. W. Hornung, creator of the 'Raffles' books – misprinted in the local newspaper report as 'E. W. Hooming'. Jerome was a scorer and the Idlers won.*

The footlights
Holmes takes to the stage

In 1893, the detective was translated to the theatre – in musical parody form. The play entitled *Under the Clock – or Sheerluck: An Extravaganza, in One Act –* was mounted at London's Royal Court Theatre in November. C. H. E. (Charles) Brookfield co-wrote it and played Holmes, thus becoming the first known professional actor to portray the great detective.

Soon after came a play, in five acts, by a minor dramatist called Charles Rogers. Under the title *Sherlock Holmes, Private Detective*, it had received what was known as a 'copyright performance' in Hanley (now part of Stoke-on-Trent) in December 1892. At least one such performance had to be put on in those days to establish rights to its author before a full production was launched. Which it duly was, in Glasgow in May 1894. This play has been described as 'a lurid melodrama in the accepted style of the period' and the Glasgow *Evening Citizen* recommended that 'nervous people should not go to see *Sherlock Holmes*'.

Enter William Gillette

However something far more important began brewing in Arthur Conan Doyle's mind in 1897: the idea that he himself should put his creation on stage. He sketched out a drama and sent it to the greatest actor of the day, Herbert Beerbohm Tree, to see if he was interested in pursuing the project. He was, but only if a few more 'Treeisms' were put in at the expense of Holmes' real character. Conan Doyle balked at this, but the concept was now out in the open. Subsequently a very successful American leading man and playwright, William Gillette, approached Conan Doyle via the theatrical impresario Charles Frohman with a view to using the character himself. Although the deal, for obvious publicity and rights purposes, would be that any resulting play would have Conan Doyle's name on it as well as his own, it was always clear that the work would effectively be Gillette's.

That deal was made, and Conan Doyle wrote excitedly and materialistically to his mother that the play 'promises to be a very big thing.

William Gillette

My agent says there are thousands of pounds in it. It will appear in New York with Gillette as Holmes. So we are cheerful. But no chickens have been either hatched or counted. Only a couple of palpable eggs.' William Gillette wrote a famous letter to the author, asking if he could 'marry' Holmes; back came the more famous answer: 'You may marry him, murder him, or do what you like to him.' In autumn 1898, fire destroyed Gillette's nearly complete manuscript, but he simply re-wrote it and presented it to Conan Doyle for his final approval in the spring of 1899.

Conan Doyle became excited in a June 1899 letter to his mother: 'Gillette has made a great play out of it, and he is a great actor, and bar some unforeseen event before October, when it will be produced in America, I am sure that it is destined for success, and if it once starts well it will go on running in many companies for many years. It has such an enormous initial advertisement. I am not usually over sanguine but I do have great hopes for this. It is our trump card.' The 'advertisement' he mentions was the name of Sherlock Holmes; the 'trump card' a financial one.

Conan Doyle was, however, writing with a certain degree of knowledge of what might be: six days earlier, the play had had its copyright performance at the Duke of York's Theatre in London. The play, above the names 'Arthur Conan Doyle and William Gillette' was titled, quite simply, *Sherlock Holmes – A Drama in Four Acts*. It turned out to be a stunning success over the next three decades, and its revival in London by the Royal Shakespeare Company in 1974 was a major contributing factor to the Sherlock Holmes popularity boom that continues to this day.

GILLETTE'S BACKGROUND

William Hooker Gillette (see 'The footlights') was born in Connecticut in 1853 and probably first appeared on stage in 1875. The first play he wrote, a comedy entitled **The Professor,** *opened six years later. Gillette was to establish immediately, both as an actor and a dramatist, a presence that relied on realism, a key dramatic innovation at the time. A review of his greatest success prior to* **Sherlock Holmes** *– the American Civil War play,* **Secret Service** *– highlighted this in critical form: 'He carries to an extreme that air of imperturbability and unconcern…Mr Gillette's method has, perhaps, the merit of originality, but it is hardly high art. He is also almost inaudible at times in his strained efforts to appear cool.' While inaudibility from the stage is fairly criminal, a recent biography –* **William Gillette,**

America's Sherlock Holmes *by Henry Zecher – makes it clear that this reserve was a quite deliberate approach by Gillette to distance himself from habitual melodramatic antics on the Victorian stage. He achieved success with two other plays* – **Too Much Johnson** *and* **Held By The Enemy** *– before taking over the Holmes territory. He was, by 1899, a very big stage star on both sides of the Atlantic, and 46 years old. William Gillette was some decades older when he finally gave up playing the character of Holmes.*

Sherlock Holmes
The play that became Gillette's greatest success

The play *Sherlock Holmes* opened in Buffalo, New York, in October 1899. The local newspaper reviewers immediately spotted the reasons for inevitable success – while hardly raving about the plot itself: '[T]he hand of the actor-dramatist is seen everywhere. Where his own personality as an actor does not suffice, his stagecraft comes to the rescue.'; '…Holmes, trapped in a cellar, and surrounded by four of the worst of villains after his life, not only walks out unharmed, but takes with him a defenceless girl, and caps the climax by laughing "Ha! Ha!" at the disconcerted criminals when they discover his escape. One forgets that such a scene is nonsensical, and becomes fully as interested as the boys in the gallery, who were so excited that they forgot to hiss the villain.'

The play moved to the Garrick Theatre on Broadway, where it ran for 236 performances until the following June. A review of the opening night's show relieves one of the necessity of providing the full plot: 'If ever there was a…thriller, we got it at the Garrick last night in *Sherlock Holmes*…[Y]ou were plunged through a thick detective atmosphere to creepy music, "dark" stages, and all the necessaries of rampant melodrama. Threats of death, exploits in circular stairways, long tunnels, underground dens, a thrilling escape from the Stepney Gas Chamber, and introductions to criminals of all sorts and descriptions made you sit up and wonder where you were.' The *New York Herald* was more practical in its praise: the play 'was so capitally written, so admirably worked out in its dramatic effects, was so impossible and yet so intensely interesting, that we all enjoyed it immensely, and after the last act called Mr Gillette out to receive the warmest sort of congratulations.'

The history of the play and Gillette's success in it is one of those theatrical tales that could not possibly be replicated today – apart, of course, for the phenomenon that is Agatha Christie's *The Mousetrap*. Gillette and Charles Frohman brought it over to London in September 1901, where it ran for 216 performances. When it once again returned to Britain in 1905, the part of Billy the page was famously played by a young Charles Chaplin. Over the years, Gillette took occasional breaks, but he embarked on a *final* final tour with the play in November 1929, bringing the curtain down in February 1932 at the age of 78. It was, incidentally, Gillette who introduced the concept of the curved

William Gillette as Holmes

calabash as Holmes' favoured pipe: it was easier, he said, to declaim lines with such a pipe in his mouth than the usual straight-stemmed one.

THE PLAY WENT ON
An American company filmed Gillette in **Sherlock Holmes** *in 1916, but no copy of this work is known to exist. One year before his death in 1937, Gillette was recorded performing a scene from the play by a Boston professor on a fragile glass*

cylinder – and those nine minutes do still exist. Orson Welles and his Mercury Theatre of the Air radio company performed the show on CBS radio in September 1938, a month before their rather more famous **War of the Worlds** broadcast. In Britain, Charles Frohman sent out various touring companies to perform **Sherlock Holmes** for years. However in 1973, a brave decision was made by the Royal Shakespeare Company to revive this by now elderly play and it was launched at the Aldwych Theatre on 1 January 1974, with John Wood playing Holmes and a young Tim Piggott-Smith as Watson. It was a triumph and became a major contribution in renewing Sherlock Holmes to the acquaintanceship of the masses. When this production travelled to Broadway, actors such as John Neville and Robert Stephens played the lead.

The Hound looms
The return of the detective

In 1900 Conan Doyle travelled to South Africa, to work as a volunteer surgeon and pull together material for his history, *The Great Boer War*. While there, he met and struck up a friendship with a journalist named Bertram Fletcher Robinson, a man without whom *The Hound of the Baskervilles*, the most famous of the Sherlock Holmes adventures, would never have been written. Moreover, it was not even originally intended to be a Holmes story, the author having effectively killed the detective in 1893 (see 'Reichenbach beckoned').

In the spring of 1901, Conan Doyle and Robinson played golf together at Cromer in Norfolk, the result of which Conan Doyle communicated to his mother in a letter from the hotel at which they were staying: 'Fletcher Robinson came here with me and we are going to do a small book together "The Hound of the Baskervilles" – a real Creeper.' It transpired that Robinson had told the author of a Devon folk tale about a spectral hound on

Dartmoor, Devon

Dartmoor which had caught Conan Doyle's imagination. The idea was quickly sold to Greenhough Smith at *The Strand Magazine*, with the stipulation that Fletcher would have to be paid as well for the idea. Conan Doyle started to work hard on the tale, but had no central lead character.

He had never entirely closed off the idea of Sherlock Holmes returning since the character's demise at Reichenbach Falls and, of course, his great creation was much on his mind in 1901 because of the Gillette play (see '*Sherlock Holmes*').

The suggestion that Holmes should appear in the story was made to *The Strand* and the payment for the story was immediately increased – to £100 per 1,000 words. Conan Doyle and Robinson were driven around Dartmoor by Robinson's 17-year-old coachman, William Henry ('Harry') Baskerville. The dating of the case was carefully chosen to imply that the new adventure must have taken place before Moriarty and the Reichenbach – so it could not quite be construed as a true 'return'.

Conan Doyle wrote quickly and

the first instalment appeared in the August edition of *The Strand*. The tale begins with a classic deduction sequence examining a visitor's walking stick, and then moves quickly back two centuries to a story of rakish behaviour, a mistreated maiden and some ripped-out throats. This was the first time Conan Doyle had written one Sherlock Holmes adventure over monthly instalments, and thus a cliffhanger ending each time was vital. There has never been a better one in popular literature than that which closed instalment No. 1.

The client, Dr Mortimer, is describing to Holmes the discovery of a body at Baskerville Hall, made by the family butler: ' "But one false statement was made by Barrymore at the inquest. He said that there were no traces upon the ground round the body. He did not observe any. But I did – some little distance off, but fresh and clear." "Footprints?" "Footprints." "A man's or a woman's?" Dr Mortimer looked strangely at us for an instant, and his voice sank almost to a whisper as he answered. "Mr Holmes, they were the footprints of a gigantic hound!" ' '

The final episode appeared in the April 1902 edition of *The Strand*, by which time the publishers had printed 25,000 copies of a book edition at 6 shillings a copy. This volume is now one of the most sought-after of editions for collectors. Whether or not Conan Doyle wished it, Sherlock Holmes was back, for the duration.

THE HOUND EXTRAS

When bound as a single volume, The Hound of the Baskervilles was published with a dust jacket; one of these had not been seen for years until an auction in 1998 threw up a first edition with one still intact. The volume alone would have attracted a price of £2,000 to £3,000, yet this one with dust jacket sold for £80,000. Could this be the most expensive dust jacket ever? How Conan Doyle permitted it one cannot guess, but many pages of his original manuscript were sent out to bookshops for publicity purposes when The Hound was published in the USA. Only 35 such separate pages are still known to exist. Harry Baskerville (see 'The Hound looms') died in 1966 – his

memorial stone may be seen in the St Pancras Church graveyard in Widecombe-on-the-Moor, Devon. A rather special first edition of **The Hound,** *inscribed to Harry by Fletcher Robinson, has not been seen for a long time.*

It was inevitable
The story of the real return

In 1903, Conan Doyle's main literary priority was writing his first series of stories about Brigadier Gerard, his exuberant Napoleonic officer of hussars and the second of the author's three great creations. The third was Professor Challenger; if *The Lost World* (1912) had never been written, we would never have had the film *Jurassic Park*. For these stories Conan Doyle was to receive £50 per 1,000 words but, as he said to Greenhough Smith at *The Strand Magazine*, 'Sherlock is another question. But he won't come up so far as I can see.'

However Sherlock did come up, as he was always going to. *The Hound of the Baskervilles* had re-established

the detective in the public's psyche and the pressure was on for his full return. The catalyst came from the US magazine publishers Collier's when they offered $25,000 for six new stories, $30,000 for eight or $45,000 for 13 (Conan Doyle provided the latter). It should be noted that the prevailing exchange rate was $4.86 to the pound. This was for US rights only; he was to receive at least £500 per story for the first six from *The Strand*. 'I don't see why I should not have another go at them,' Conan Doyle wrote to his mother, 'and earn three times as much money as I can by any other form of work. I have finished the first one…and it is a rare good one. You will find that Holmes was never dead, and that he is now very much alive.'

And so it was that readers of *Collier's Weekly* in the USA and *The Strand* in Britain enjoyed the opening words to 'The Empty House' in their respective magazines in October 1903: 'It was in the spring of the year 1894 that all London was interested, and the fashionable world dismayed, by the murder of the Honourable Ronald Adair, under most unusual

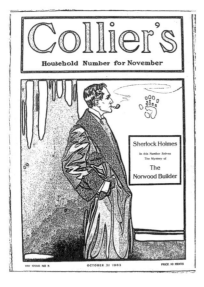

Four sentences from his account to Watson have provided untold ammunition for Holmes 'scholars' ever since: 'I travelled for two years in Tibet, therefore, and amused myself by visiting Lhasa and spending some days with the head Lama. You may have read of the remarkable explorations of a Norwegian named Sigerson, but I am sure that it never occurred to you that you were receiving news of your friend. I then passed through Persia, looked in at Mecca, and paid a short but interesting visit to the Khalifa at Khartoum, the results of which I have communicated to the Foreign Office. Returning to France, I spent some months in a research into the coal-tar derivatives, which I conducted in a laboratory at Montpellier, in the south of France.' The basic errors committed by Conan Doyle in writing these few sentences are too detailed to explore here.

and inexplicable circumstances.' Holmes duly reappears, causing Dr Watson to faint, and then it is almost business as usual, although the detective has to spend much time explaining how he hadn't actually died in Switzerland and why he had been away from London for three years. Essentially, the reason he gave for his absence was that not all the Moriarty gang had been rounded up and he was afraid for his life if he returned too soon.

FREDERIC DORR STEELE
It was with the return of Holmes in **Collier's** *magazine (see 'It was inevitable') that the second great illustrator of the stories stepped up.*

Dorr Steele, aged 30 in 1903, had worked for **Scribner's Magazine.** *When asked to provide artwork for the new Holmes stories, he made a very sensible decision: to use as his muse the greatest star in the USA to play Holmes, William Gillette. Steele's work is more impressionistic than that of Sidney Paget; he made fewer illustrations and also did not provide the homely touch of Paget. Yet it is Steele's interpretation of his subject that is probably better known today. Especially since he was granted a significant bonus: Steele was asked to complete magnificent colour illustrations for the covers of the Holmes editions of the magazine, the results of which are very striking. Paget had never been given such an opportunity. Steele attended the first dinner of the US Baker Street Irregulars fan club in 1934, and had embarked on a project to provide new illustrations for all the Sherlock Holmes tales – he had, by definition, missed working on three long stories and the first 24 short ones – when he died in 1944.*

The Return of Sherlock Holmes
Short story breakdown, Part 2

The following are my précis of the 13 plot lines in *The Return of Sherlock Holmes*:

THE EMPTY HOUSE: Reunion with Watson, resolution of Moriarty story, good London geography.

THE NORWOOD BUILDER: Excellent Baker Street client entrance, seemingly complex mystery, vital thumbprint clue, creepy South London villain, was there really a crime committed?

THE SOLITARY CYCLIST: Surrey location, classic frightened female client with romantic attachments, solid what's-going-on mystery, a shooting but no crime.

THE DANCING MEN: Great code mystery, Norfolk location, American historical backdrop, murder.

THE PRIORY SCHOOL: Peak District location, wide-ranging plot involving abduction, murder and bicycle tracks, interesting class elements throughout, big payoff for Holmes.

BLACK PETER: Marvellous murder story in Sussex location, good strong villain, important appearance by detective Stanley Hopkins (liked by Holmes), midnight vigil, surprising resolution.

CHARLES AUGUSTUS MILVERTON: Classic London location (Hampstead), oily and evil blackmailer, passion, revenge and a shooting, Holmes becomes engaged to be married.

THE SIX NAPOLEONS: London-based curiosity of a plot, genuine detective work required, murder en passant, fine dramatic resolution.

THE THREE STUDENTS: Exam-cheating mystery in 'Camford' (Cambridge), no crime as such, pleasant tale carelessly written, important in the Oxford-Cambridge controversy.

THE GOLDEN PINCE-NEZ: Kent location, second appearance by Inspector Stanley Hopkins, one very basic deductive process employed, unsatisfactory characterisations, murder with historical background.

THE MISSING THREE-QUARTER: Another university-based mystery (definitely Cambridge), make-weight story with no crime but some personal sadness.

THE ABBEY GRANGE: Cracking opening, Kent location, murder, passion, critical wine-based detective work, a classic.

THE SECOND STAIN: Back to London, plot involves politicians and possible international intrigue, no crime, intriguing finish.

The start of scholarship
Something new in detective fiction

In 1902, a young student at Cambridge University published an article in *The Cambridge Review* entitled '*The Hound of the Baskervilles at Fault*'. The student, Frank Sidgwick (who later founded the famous publishing firm of Sidgwick & Jackson), formulated his paper as an open letter to Dr Watson and posed a few difficult and practical questions regarding dates in the adventure that didn't quite add up. An irrevocable step had been taken. No piece of crime fiction had previously been subjected to pseudo-scholarly investigation, and while the floodgates did not truly open for another 30 years or so, Sidgwick must take his place in the footnotes of Sherlock Holmes literary history.

On the other side of the Atlantic, Arthur Bartlett Maurice was assistant–editor at *The Bookman*, a New York-based journal, also writing on Holmesian themes in the same year. He pointed out how Watson had once said that Holmes' knowledge of literature had been 'nil', after which the detective soon made all sorts of literary quotes; he also criticised elements in *The Hound of the Baskervilles*. Again in 1902, a contributor to a lawyer's journal in Boston wrote heavily: 'Looking at them in the mass…the writer is led to the conviction that were the incidents on which they are exercised made to run the gauntlet of the rules of evidence, nearly all of Holmes' dialectic efforts would fall short of actual demonstration of the point to be settled in each case.'

Back in London in 1904, the critic Andrew Lang asked some questions about the story called 'The Three Students' in *Longman's Magazine*. At this time, it was less of a wave and more a ripple, but those publishing magazines covering

Arthur Bartlett Maurice

popular literature were latching on to an enthusiasm for background Sherlock Holmes material. This was eventually to lead to the founding of groups such as the Baker Street Irregulars in the USA and the Sherlock Holmes Society of London.

The bright
Ronald Knox
'Studies in the Literature of
Sherlock Holmes'

On Friday 10 March 1911, a
young Oxford don named
Ronald Knox read a paper to a group
of undergraduates at Merton College
who gathered under the name of the
Bodley Club. The Club was a literary
society devoted to reading and
discussion. Knox was 23 years old and
a Fellow – soon to be Chaplain – of
another college, Trinity.

Terrifyingly bright, Knox wished
to bring satire to bear on 'Higher
Criticism', the contemporary study of
the Bible that invited erudite scholars
and their sometimes overblown and
pretentious conclusions. Knox was,
for example, intrigued by German
scholars who worried why the
gospels of both Matthew and Mark
related the death of John the Baptist
as a flashback – and thus what this
might mean, or imply, about the
authorship of the gospels.

Knox identified Sherlock Holmes
as a vehicle for making subtle fun
of this approach to scholarship. In

Ronald Knox

doing so, entirely unintentionally,
he laid the foundation stone –
in the footsteps of Sidgwick,
Maurice and Lang (see 'The start
of scholarship') – for the study of
matters Holmesian. His satire, 'Studies
in the Literature of Sherlock Holmes',
was extraordinary, and his style rings
true to this day in terms of criticising
pretention in literary matters.

This quote from the work sums up
his approach: '[T]he seal, and symbol,
and secret of Watson is, of course, his

bowler. It is not like other bowlers: it is a priestly vestment, an *insigne* of office. Holmes may wear a squash hat, but Watson cleaves to his bowler, even at midnight in the silence of Dartmoor, or on the solitary slopes of the Reichenbach. He wears it constantly, even as the archimandrite or the rabbi wears his hat: to remove it would be akin to the shearing of Samson's locks by Delilah. "Watson and his bowler," says M. Piff-Pouff, "they are separable only in thought." It is his apex of wool, his *petasus* of invisibility, his *mitra pretiosa*, his triple tiara, his halo.'

Piff-Pouff, it hardly needs to be pointed out, is an invented fake scholar. Yet what Knox also did was to raise all sorts of questions that people have enjoyed so much over the years and to contribute to the pleasure given decades later by the Ritchie films and the BBC's *Sherlock*. He asks which university Holmes attended; he is the first to highlight the fact that Watson's wife calls him by the wrong Christian name in one story; and he spots different colours of Holmes' dressing gown, as variously described by Watson.

This is where the fun started. Knox's paper was first published in 1912, but most importantly appeared in a 1928 collection of his various pieces under the title *Essays in Satire*. It was reviewed a year later by S. C. (Sidney Castle) Roberts in the *Cambridge Review,* who went on to have much fun in published form about Dr Watson, to join the first, short-lived, Sherlock Holmes Society in 1934 and to be made President of the Sherlock Holmes Society of London upon its foundation in 1951.

KNOX AND CONAN DOYLE

Ronald Knox sent a copy of his paper to Conan Doyle in 1912; amazingly, he received a letter of thanks. It is one of the few examples of the author writing in private about his greatest creation and is delightfully revealing, beginning as follows: 'I cannot help writing to you to tell you of the amusement – and also the amazement – with which I read your article on Sherlock Holmes. That anyone should spend such pains on such material was what surprised me. Certainly you know a great deal more

about it than I do, for the stories have been written in a disconnected (and careless) way, without referring back to what had gone before. I am only pleased that you have not found more discrepancies, especially as to dates.'

Baffled!
Holmes in the silent film era

In 1900, the inevitable happened: if the concept of narrative film existed, then Sherlock Holmes was bound to be brought in on the act. Indeed it was the stage success of William Gillette (see '*Sherlock Holmes*') that most certainly led to the first ever cinematic presentation – silent, of course – which used the name of the detective to sell 49 seconds or so of clever (for then) stop-action photography.

The film was called *Sherlock Holmes Baffled* and the unnamed actor playing Holmes wears a character-identifying dressing gown, smokes a cigar and tries to see off a burglar who constantly disappears and then reappears elsewhere. Made by the US Mutoscope and Biograph Company, it was filmed in the USA and made for peep-show machines. As Michael Pointer writes in *The Public Life of Sherlock Holmes* (1975): '[T]he film was a mildly amusing little piece, easily understood by the general public of the day. It is important only in that it marks the first use on film of the name and the character Sherlock Holmes.'

The next important Holmes films came, perhaps surprisingly, from Scandinavia, with a series of 11 made from 1908 to 1911 by the Nordisk Film Company in Denmark. The actor Viggo Larsen played Holmes in six of the films – as well as writing and directing them. Although none of the films are known to have survived, available synopses do show that recognisable vignettes from the real tales were written in.

Éclair
Conan Doyle received no payment for the use of his character in any of the very early films. However in 1911 a French company, Éclair, made a deal with the author to make eight films, all of which were to be reasonably faithful adaptations of his stories.

Sherlock Holmes Baffled *(1900)*

Filmed in Bexhill-on-Sea, they had British casts – apart from Holmes himself, who was played by a French actor, Georges Treville.

The company must have been confident of the film's success, if their advertising is anything to go by: 'Only One Producer in the World could Obtain It. Only One Producer in the World could Perfect It. Éclair obtained and perfected SHERLOCK HOLMES by Sir Arthur Conan Doyle. The Greatest Detective Tale in the World. The Most Thrilling Character in Literature', and so on.

Conan Doyle's mention of the series in his autobiography was brief and typically pithy: '[W]hen these rights were finally discussed and a small sum offered for them by a French Company it seemed treasure trove and I was very glad to accept. Afterwards I had to buy them back again at exactly ten times what I had received, so the deal was a disastrous one.'

Stoll

The most notable Sherlock Holmes films to be made in the silent era was an incredible series of 47, produced by the Stoll Company in Britain from 1920 to 1923. Each one of them was a reasonably faithful adaptation of a story – apart from the fact they were all firmly set in the 1920s – and starred the stage actor Eille Norwood as Holmes. He was nearly 60 when he took on the role and would not be remembered today had it not been for this casting.

Yet he certainly thought seriously about the rôle: 'My idea of Holmes,' he wrote, 'is that he is absolutely quiet. Nothing ruffles him but he is a man who intuitively seizes on points without revealing that he has done so, and nurses them up with complete inaction until the moment when he is called upon to exercise his wonderful detective powers. Then he is like a cat – the person he is after is the only person in all the world,

and he is oblivious of everything else till his quarry is run to earth.'

Conan Doyle was a fan of Norwood's portrayal of Holmes in the films and reinforced the importance of imperturbability in the character: 'He has that rare quality which can only be described as glamour, which compels you to watch an actor even when he is doing nothing. He has the brooding eye which excites expectation and he has also a quite unrivalled power of disguise.'

It was at a big publicity dinner held by Stoll in 1921, attended by Norwood, Greenough Smith of *The Strand Magazine* and popular writers such as A. E. W. Mason and Edgar Wallace, that Conan Doyle first told the story of an event that had brought home to him Holmes' popularity: 'I think of all the little incidents that have pleased me in connection with Holmes was when a party of schoolboys from the Paris lycées were [sic] brought to London, crammed into charabancs; asked what they would like to see first, and, when everybody thought they would say Westminster Abbey, all replied "Baker Street".'

Sherlock Holmes

There was one more silent film of note. It came out in 1922 and was entitled, simply, *Sherlock Holmes* (released as *Moriarty* in Britain to avoid interference with the film rights owned by the Stoll Company). Starring the hugely popular Hollywood actor John Barrymore, it was a treatment of the original William Gillette play. The director, Albert Parker, remembered huge rows with his lead actor throughout the filming in London, Switzerland and California – mostly due to Barrymore's drinking.

Barrymore himself has left a delightful memory of his Watson, played by Roland Young: 'I suggested a little stage business now and then, so that such a charming, agreeable thespian might not be altogether lost in the shuffle. When I saw the completed film, I was flabbergasted, stunned, and almost became an atheist on the spot. That quiet, agreeable bastard had stolen, not one, but every damned scene!…He is such a splendid gentleman in real life, but what a cunning, larcenous demon when on the boards!'

In any event, sound films were just around the corner and with them the defining cinema double act of Basil Rathbone and Nigel Bruce (see 'The talkies' and 'Rathbone arrives').

Output dwindles
The story of writing
His Last Bow

The 'last' Holmes short story, 'The Second Stain', had been published in December 1904. And the collection entitled *The Return of Sherlock Holmes* – the last Sherlock Holmes volume to publish, incidentally, under the imprint of George Newnes & Co. – had appeared the following year.

The opening lines of 'The Second Stain' could not have been more explicit in indicating what Conan Doyle was still intending to do to his hero. As he had Watson write: 'I had intended "The Adventure of the Abbey Grange" to be the last of those exploits of my friend, Mr Sherlock Holmes, which I should ever communicate to the public…So long as he was in actual professional practice the records of his successes were of some practical value to him; but since he has definitely retired from London and betaken him to study and bee-farming on the Sussex Downs, notoriety has become hateful to him…'

In 1906 Conan Doyle's wife, Louise, passed away, having suffered from tuberculosis for 13 years. She left him with their two teenage children: Mary, born in 1889, and Kingsley, born in 1892. Her death left him able to formalise his relationship – most likely to have been platonic – with Jean Leckie, whom he had met nine years earlier. They married a year later and she was to bear him a further three children. In 1906 also, he published one of the medieval romances for which he originally believed he would be most remembered: entitled *Sir Nigel*, it was a tale of derring-do and a prequel to his novel *The White Company* (1891). There had not been much time or inclination on the part of Conan Doyle for Sherlock Holmes; yet the pressure, as always, was on.

A long-drawn-out process

On 4 March 1908, Conan Doyle wrote to Greenhough Smith at *The Strand Magazine* with such lackadaisical boredom that he repeated one of his famous mistakes regarding Watson's forename: 'I don't suppose so far as I can see that I should write a new "Sherlock Holmes" series but I see no reason why I should not do an occasional scattered story under some such heading as "Reminiscences of Mr Sherlock Holmes" (extracted from the Diaries of his friend, Dr James Watson). I have one pretty clear in my head & this I think really will mature. If you could fix it with Watt it might do for your Midsummer number & perhaps I could dig out another for your Christmas number.' Moreover, a month later he wrote to his mother: 'I have done a new Holmes Story. I intend to do one other. They won't be so bad as to hurt my reputation & the money will be useful.'

However lugubrious about the affair he sounded, Conan Doyle knew perfectly well that the magazine would leap at the commercial prospect – for itself and its sales – of two new Holmes stories in prime-month issues. For himself, he was all too aware that he would make a great deal of money if his agent, Watt, did the job properly. In the event, the US magazine *Collier's Weekly* also ended up paying some £750 for each of the stories.

However this was to be a long-drawn-out process, as Conan Doyle had implied. The first of the new bunch of stories, 'Wisteria Lodge', was, in the event, spread over the two *Strand* issues for September and October, with the second, 'The Bruce-Partington Plans', occupying, as the author had suggested, the Christmas issue. Then there was a two-year gap until the next appeared, and only two further stories in 1911, one of them again a two-parter.

The public then waited until December 1913 for another, and – believe it or not – until September 1917 for what was to be the final entry in the collection published as *His Last Bow*. This collection had thus turned out to be a long nine-year stretch in the making.

THE VALLEY OF FEAR

Conan Doyle took nine years to write the collection **His Last Bow** *(see 'Output dwindles'). It should be pointed out, however, that the First World War intervened, Conan Doyle making several visits to France, and he did take the time during that period to pen what was to be the last of his long stories starring the detective,* **The Valley of Fear**. *As with* **A Study in Scarlet**, *the actual Sherlockian element of the tale sandwiched an American historical central portion, this time dealing with the true story of the outrages that took place in the Pennsylvanian coalfields in the 1870s, and the infiltration by a police agent of a murderous miners' group. The author's eye was undoubtedly on the US market. There is a fine piece of deduction at the start (from what book can a coded message have been created?) and there is a remote, but pleasing, Professor Moriarty presence.*

His Last Bow
Short story breakdown, Part 3

The following are my précis of the 7 plot lines in *His Last Bow*:

WISTERIA LODGE: Two parts, unnecessary length, cheap thrills in the Home Counties, a murder with grotesque overtones.

THE BRUCE-PARTINGTON PLANS: One of the best short stories, murder, Government security, spies, submarines, an invaluable perspective of the London Underground, plus a welcome reappearance of Mycroft.

THE DEVIL'S FOOT: Murder and madness in Cornwall, passion at the heart of the plot, Holmes and Watson bond in poisonous circumstances, thoroughly satisfactory.

THE RED CIRCLE: One of the worst short stories, utterly not worth its two-part length, murder in London, Mafia overtones, no subtlety.

THE DISAPPEARANCE OF LADY FRANCES CARFAX: A bit of France, mostly London, nearly murder, nasty pair of villains, reasonable deduction to solve a deep mystery.

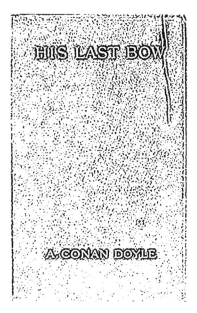

THE DYING DETECTIVE: One of a kind, no hints. For information: this was the one Sherlock Holmes story illustrated in *The Strand Magazine* by Sidney Paget's brother, Walter.

HIS LAST BOW: Told in the third person, set at the outbreak of the First World War and presages future war propaganda use of Sherlock Holmes (in films), no crime as such apart from dastardly espionage.

THE GREAT WAR

*The short story 'His Last Bow'
has a great example of valedictory
writing by Conan Doyle at its close.
Holmes and Watson (for the first
time I give the plot away) have dealt
with a leading German spy and are
preparing for what will surely come
after 2 August 1914 – the specific date
Conan Doyle allocates to the story
(Britain, of course, declared war two
days later). The quotation follows:
' "There's an east wind coming,
Watson." "I think not, Holmes. It is
very warm." "Good old Watson! You
are the one fixed point in a changing
age. There's an east wind coming all
the same, such a wind as never blew
on England yet. It will be cold and
bitter, Watson, and a good many of us
may wither before its blast. But it's
God's own wind none the less, and
a cleaner, better, stronger land will
lie in the sunshine when the storm
has cleared." ' Conan Doyle's son,
Kingsley, was wounded serving on
the Western Front, and died in 1918
during the post-war flu pandemic
from a condition aggravated by his
injuries. Conan Doyle's younger
brother, Innes, was a Brigadier-
General in the war and also died in
the flu pandemic, a year later.*

Post Gillette's masterpiece
More Holmes on stage, Part 1

Although William Gillette's play *Sherlock Holmes* is the most important dramatic representation of the detective (see 'The footlights' and '*Sherlock Holmes*'), Holmes has trodden the boards in numerous forms over the years. Most outings have been adaptations of stories – or thematic pull-togethers that convey the atmosphere of the tales – but there have also been one-man shows, musicals and even a ballet (see also 'Up to date').

One of the most unusual stage presentations came again from Gillette. In 1905, he brought to London a new comedy entitled *Clarice* and decided that it needed a curtain-raiser – some short entertainment to stretch the evening. The result was *The Painful Predicament of Sherlock Holmes*, subtitled 'A

Fantasy – in about one-tenth of an act'. Gillette tested it in New York for one performance, as part of a benefit: he himself played Holmes, of course, with the young Ethel Barrymore as a rather distraught client named Gwendolyn Cobb, and Henry McArdle reprising his role as Billy the pageboy from the original *Sherlock Holmes*. On its move to London a successful British comedy actress, Irene Vanbrugh, took over the client role, and someone who was to become famous comically in his own right played Billy – a certain 'Master Charles Chaplin'.

The playlet itself is not important but for the fact that Holmes speaks not one word throughout, while Miss Cobb talks incessantly and somewhat wildly. At one point Holmes scribbles something on a piece of paper and passes it to Billy, who then exits. He soon returns with two uniformed men, who escort the lady off stage. Billy closes the show with the grave statement: 'It was the *right* asylum, sir!'

Five years later, a dramatisation by Conan Doyle of his novel about 18th century boxing, *Rodney Stone*, closed at a London theatre on which the

author held a six month lease and, as he said, '[A]n empty theatre spells ruin.' So Conan Doyle did what he did best: he wrote something very quickly indeed. The result was a stage version of his great Holmes short story 'The Speckled Band', opening in June 1910 with H. A. Saintsbury as Holmes and a leading character actor of the time, Lyn Harding, as the unaccountably misspelt villain Dr Grimesby Rylott (in the published story, it's 'Roylott'). A snake played a vital part in the production and Conan Doyle was rather pleased with it: 'We had a fine rock boa to play the title-role, a snake which was the pride of my heart, so one can imagine my disgust when I saw that one critic ended his disparaging review by the words "The crisis of the play was produced by the appearance of a palpably artificial serpent." I was inclined to offer him a goodly sum if he would undertake to go to bed with it.'

In 1921, the author wrote a one-act Sherlock Holmes play called *The Crown Diamond* which only ran for a couple of weeks. Never one to miss a financial trick, Conan Doyle reversed the usual practice and turned the play into a short story (one of the worst) called 'The Mazarin Stone', which was published in *The Strand Magazine* in October that year. And off the back of his film success (see 'Baffled!'), Eille Norwood appeared in a play called *The Return of Sherlock Holmes*, which ran successfully in London and the provinces from 1923 to1924.

Spiritualism dominates
Conan Doyle and his religious beliefs

From 1919 until his death in 1930, Conan Doyle's life was dominated by his belief in, and publicity-seeking for, spiritualism. This was certainly not a new interest: he had attended lectures on psychic beliefs back in his early working days in Southsea in the 1880s. However in the aftermath of the First World War – with some 800,000 British soldiers killed or missing – there was a greater appetite than before for those who believed in such matters to attempt communication with their lost loved ones and, as a true believer and missionary for spiritualism, the author

spent much of his time travelling, lecturing and debating the issues. In this he was strongly supported by his wife Jean, who claimed to have the power of automatic writing.

Conan Doyle set up, and largely personally funded, a psychic bookshop – intriguingly, almost next door to Westminster Abbey – with the extraordinary telegraph address of 'Ectoplasm Sowest London'. Famously, he became involved in publicising the photographs taken by the young girls Frances Griffiths and Elsie Wright in Cottingley, West Yorkshire, which purported to be of fairies. It was not until the 1980s that one of the two admitted that they had faked them, but in 1920 debate raged and Conan Doyle endured some ridicule in the process.

During this period, the author pushed his beliefs in the paranormal into some of his popular writings, most obviously in two of his Professor Challenger tales. However, perhaps aware of the dangers of tampering with his most famous creation and risking outcry from his readers and a loss of sales, Conan Doyle kept Sherlock Holmes clean from such writings. Indeed, in the 1925 story 'The Sussex Vampire' – written at the very height of his spiritualism crusade – he actually has Holmes say: 'This agency stands flat-footed upon the ground and there it must remain. The world is big enough for us. No ghosts need apply.' Income from his writing during this period was duly ploughed into the psychic bookshop.

The final demise
Conan Doyle's last
decade of writing

Frances Griffiths and Elsie Wright

Dominated by his belief in Spiritualism (see 'Spiritualism dominates') Conan Doyle nevertheless continued to write during his last decade until his death in 1930, producing 12 Holmes stories between 1921 and 1927 – pulled together in the latter year as *The Casebook of Sherlock Holmes* – amongst other literary endeavours. We have a first hand description of Conan Doyle's writing practice at this time from his youngest child, Jean, born in 1912. As Editor then of *The Sherlock Holmes Journal*, I commissioned her – by then Air Commandant Dame

Jean Conan Doyle – to write some memories of her father 50 years after his death:

'I wasn't allowed to read Sherlock Holmes when I first wanted to, so, like thousands of other children, I read them by torch beneath the bed-clothes. Later on my father wrote *The Case-book of Sherlock Holmes* and we had the fun of having the stories read to us, when only half-written, during lunch, and in the evening hearing the completed story. He'd get the idea for a plot during the night, get up about six and write all morning; he always wrote in his study or in a small hut he had built in a field where he was never disturbed. He always invited criticisms, but the only ones – and they were rare – came from my mother. They were usually acted upon.'

There is little doubt that in these later stories, Conan Doyle is specifically pandering to his US readers – after all, it is reputed that his US publishers were paying him at the rate of a dollar a word by this time. Thus he has Americans as central characters in 'Thor Bridge' and 'The Three Garridebs'; and in a line that

grates on the ear, he incredibly has Holmes use the phrase 'his Grace's ma'. The author also makes clear that he no longer cared for the safe stylistic predictability which had so endeared him to readers of the Holmes stories in years gone by: three of the final 12 stories are not written by Watson.

It must be pointed out that in the story 'The Three Gables', Conan Doyle gives to Holmes and Watson a display of racist language unique in the 60 tales. Times and attitudes change and it is now shocking to see a black boxer named Steve Dixie called 'a huge negro' and 'the savage'. Holmes doesn't ask him to sit down, 'for I don't like the smell of you'; and there then follows this extraordinary piece of writing: ' "[A]ren't you Steve Dixie, the bruiser?" "That's my name, Masser Holmes, and you'll get put through it for sure if you give me any lip." "It is certainly the last thing you need," said Holmes, staring at our visitor's hideous mouth.'

Three years before his death, Conan Doyle penned a short valedictory essay, 'Mr Sherlock Holmes to his Readers', which was published in the March 1927 edition of *The Strand Magazine* and was to be slightly adapted as a preface to the book edition of *The Case-book of Sherlock Holmes* later in the year. Knowing that this time he really *was* killing Holmes off for good, Conan Doyle writes in gently lyrical terms:

'I fear that Mr Sherlock Holmes may become like one of those popular tenors who, having outlived their time, are still tempted to make repeated farewell bows to their indulgent audiences. This must cease and he must go the way of all flesh, material or imaginary…He began his adventures in the very heart of the later Victorian era, carried it through the all-too-short reign of Edward, and has managed to hold his own little niche even in these feverish days. Thus it would be true to say that those who first read of him as young men have lived to see their own grown-up children following the same adventures in the same magazine. It is a striking example of the patience and loyalty of the British public.'

STORY COMPETITION

In the March 1927 edition of **The Strand Magazine,** *readers were offered the opportunity to put in order their favourite 12 Holmes short stories (out of the 44 by then published) and to see how closely they accorded to Conan Doyle's own selection. The winner received £100, and 100 runners-up received autographed copies of the writer's autobiography. Conan Doyle's list, in order from 1 to 12, ran: 'The Speckled Band', 'The Red-Headed League', 'The Dancing Men', 'The Final Problem', 'A Scandal in Bohemia', 'The Empty House', 'The Five Orange Pips', 'The Second Stain', 'The Devil's Foot', 'The Priory School', 'The Musgrave Ritual' and 'The Reigate Squires'.*

The Case-book of Sherlock Holmes
Short story breakdown, Part 4

The following are my précis of the 12 plot lines in *The Case-book of Sherlock Holmes*:

THE MAZARIN STONE: Originally a play, written in third person, strange name of lead villain (Count Negretto Sylvius), stolen jewel, second use in stories of a bust of Holmes, first (and only) use of a gramophone.

THOR BRIDGE: Death in Hampshire, passionate affair, only mention of Watson's 'battered tin dispatch box' that contains his records of Holmes cases (thus giving rise to the opening of many a pastiche), one of the best pieces of detective work in all the stories.

THE CREEPING MAN: Weird plot unsubtly set in Camford (thus contributing to scholarly discussion of whether Holmes went to Oxford or Cambridge), strange climbing professor, no crime, best telegram of all sent to Watson: 'Come at once if convenient – if inconvenient come all the same – SH.'

THE SUSSEX VAMPIRE: Teasing title for a sad tale, no crime, clever Holmesian work helped by a mirror.

THE THREE GARRIDEBS: London-based, but US background, plot broadly similar to that of 'The Red-Headed League' although with gunshots, nice moment of tenderness between Holmes and Watson.

THE ILLUSTRIOUS CLIENT: Outright cad villain, one great female characterisation, serious physical attack on Holmes, splendid rôle-playing by Watson, sleaze but no crime.

THE THREE GABLES: Already mentioned for racial goading (see 'The final demise'), thoroughly unsatisfactory plot and characterisations.

THE BLANCHED SOLDIER: Written by Holmes with curious mention of Watson – who 'had at that time deserted me for a wife, the only selfish action which I can recall in our association' – good mystery, tragic ending, no crime in Bedfordshire.

THE LION'S MANE: Again written by Holmes, Sussex-based no-crime plot, red-herrings and, indeed, water-based rationale.

THE RETIRED COLOURMAN: South London-based, murders, good howdunnit, unpleasant villain, Watson used, and criticised, by Holmes: ' "[T]his little old home, surrounded by a high sun-baked wall, mottled with lichens and topped with moss, the sort of wall –" "Cut out the poetry, Watson," said Holmes severely. "I note that it was a high brick wall." '

THE VEILED LODGER: No crime, London-based circus plot, a bit of passion, little of interest.

SHOSCOMBE OLD PLACE: The last Sherlock Holmes story to be published (April 1927), slightly grotesque plot, horses and dead bodies but no crime.

Mystery stories
And yet another three?

Sherlock Holmes enthusiasts have always enjoyed playing games, and it has been suggested that two further stories written by Conan Doyle could be included as apocrypha to what is known, in Biblical terms, as the 'Canon'. There was another one, too, that for a short time looked as if it really was the real thing.

In July 1898, *The Strand Magazine* carried a story called 'The Story of the Man with the Watches' written by Conan Doyle. It was an entertaining and baffling tale of a murder on a train, which the police were unable to resolve. Then: 'There was a letter in the *Daily Gazette*, over the signature of a well-known criminal investigator, which gave rise to considerable discussion at the time.' There is no doubt that Conan Doyle was having fun here, phrasing the words of this 'well-known criminal investigator' just as Holmes might have done.

The very next month appeared 'The Lost Special', again involving a train and an even better mystery than the first. Curiously, Conan Doyle used the same device once more: 'Amongst the many suggestions put forward by various newspapers or private individuals, there were one or two which were feasible enough to attract the attention of the public. One which appeared in *The Times*, over the signature of an amateur reasoner of some celebrity at that date, attempted to deal with the matter in a critical and semi-scientific manner.' And this time

Conan Doyle with his son, Adrian

he added to the fun by giving this 'amateur reasoner' a sentence in the letter which any Sherlock Holmes fan would immediately have recognised: 'It is one of the elementary principles of practical reasoning that when the impossible has been eliminated the residuum, however improbable, must contain the truth.'

At this point, no true Holmes story had appeared since the end of 1893 and was not to do so again until *The Hound of the Baskervilles* started publishing in late 1901. Thus Conan Doyle was being quite clever here, giving *The Strand* readers just a frisson of recognition. And scholars merely played the game by adding these two tales to what might be called the 'Apocrypha'.

Wind on many years, to 1943, and for a short time it appeared that a real, hitherto undiscovered, Sherlock Holmes story by Arthur Conan Doyle had been identified. One of his biographers, Hesketh Pearson, had received access to family papers and mentioned something called 'The Case of the Man who was Wanted'. There was naturally huge excitement on both sides of the Atlantic at a time when there was much antagonism between Sherlock Holmes enthusiasts and those in charge of the Conan Doyle family estate – the author's two sons, Denis and Adrian. Although there were worries about its style, the story was published in the USA in August 1948 and in Britain five months later.

Then a man called Arthur Whitaker came forward, saying that many years previously he had sent Conan Doyle the written story and had received £10 for the plot. The two Conan Doyle sons fought hard to defend the story's authenticity as a genuine product written by their father, but eventually caved in to the inevitable.

The 'talkies'
The arrival of film with sound

In October 1928, the Fox Movietone News Company arranged to film an interview with Conan Doyle at his home of Windlesham in Crowborough, Sussex. The result was nearly 12 minutes of talk to a rarely moving camera in his garden, as the author sits and chatters affably in what remains a surprisingly strong Scots accent after all his years of living in England. 'Now I've got to speak one or two words to try my voice, I understand,' he begins. 'There are two things people always want to ask me' he continues; 'One of them is how I ever came to write the Sherlock Holmes stories and the other is how I came to have psychic experiences and to take so much interest in that question.'

With a very slight laugh, he begins with the Holmes side of things, mentioning his early mentor, Joseph Bell, and generally spending a few minutes in gentle and reflective memory. Towards the end, he is as firm as ever he was in print about his greatest literary character: 'I've written a good deal more about him than I ever intended to do, but my hand has been rather forced by kind friends who continually wanted to know more and so it is that this monstrous growth has come out of what was comparatively a very small seed.' And then, almost with relief, Conan Doyle moves on to 'the other point, which is of course to me the very much more serious one'.

However disparaging, it remains fascinating to see and hear the creator talking about the created; the film is now widely accessible on the internet. It should be pointed out that the first 'talkie' feature film was *The Jazz Singer*, released just a year earlier; so this Fox item is incredibly early in sound terms and a mark of how important it was thought to be to have Conan Doyle's synchronised words and pictures laid down on film for posterity.

The first Sherlock Holmes sound film didn't come along until 1929. Made by Paramount and directed (mostly) by Basil Dean, it was entitled *The Return of Sherlock Holmes* and starred a matinée idol named Clive Brook. Dean became unhappy and

Clive Brook

left, leaving Brook to complete the directorial duties himself: 'I very much enjoyed Holmes. I characterised him larger than life and this permitted much comedy. The versions of Sherlock Holmes I've seen seem inclined to make him a clever solver of crimes but gave little to his foibles and eccentricities. As far as I'm concerned Conan Doyle in his stories certainly made Holmes larger than life; and that's how I played it.'

A much greater star-to-be was lined up the following year to play Holmes: Raymond Massey appeared in *The Speckled Band* – with the shrewd choice of Lyn Harding as (still misspelt) Rylott, who had played the rôle on stage with H. A. Saintsbury two decades earlier. And a barely-remembered *Hound of the Baskervilles* came out in 1932 for Gainsborough Pictures: Robert Rendel looked nothing like anyone's impression of Holmes, but the picture did at least benefit from 'additional dialogue' provided by the immensely popular writer Edgar Wallace.

ARTHUR WONTNER

Arthur Wontner, on the other hand, looked as if he could have stepped out of the pages of **The Strand Magazine.** *He played Holmes in a hugely successful series of five British films in the early 1930s, all true to character and mostly based on original stories:* **The Sleeping Cardinal, The Missing Rembrandt, The Sign of Four, The Triumph of Sherlock Holmes** *and* **Silver Blaze.** *His Watson was a very suave actor named Ian Fleming, but guess who played Professor Moriarty in both the last two films? None other than the 'Rylott' expert, Lyn Harding (see "The 'talkies' ")! Wontner's success with the Holmes character was such*

Arthur Wontner as Holmes

that an American critic wrote: 'No other Sherlock Holmes is genuine – accept no substitute.' An additional note for film enthusiasts: in the 1953 gentle comedy classic, **Genevieve,** *John Gregson and Dinah Sheridan are nearly winning their car race back to London from Brighton when they are stopped by an elderly gentleman asking about the make of their vehicle. This gentleman is played by Arthur Wontner.*

Basil Rathbone as Holmes

Rathbone arrives
A triumph before typecasting

Even today, more than 70 years since he first appeared on screen as Holmes, Basil Rathbone remains the actor most associated with the rôle cinematically. Previously he had enjoyed huge success as a film villain – often in swashbuckling roles, and paramountly as Sir Guy of Gisbourne in the 1938 film *The Adventures of Robin Hood* – and his aquiline looks made him an easy choice to play Sherlock Holmes for Twentieth Century Fox in 1938. The idea, apparently, came at a dinner party held by the film company's boss, Daryll F. Zanuck, who enquired as to who should be Holmes. One of his leading producers and writers, Gene Markey, was to answer 'Basil Rathbone – who else?'

Signed up as Watson for the film was a second-rank character actor and pillar of the British community in Hollywood, Nigel Bruce. In his unpublished memoirs, Bruce tells how he had just been involved in a Broadway failure when he received a message: 'The telegram was from Basil Rathbone who said: "Do come back to Hollywood, Willie dear boy, and play Doctor Watson to my Sherlock Holmes. We'll have great fun together." Basil can never realise how much that telegram cheered me up, as when I received it, I was in the mood to put my head in a gas oven.' Together, these two men formed a partnership that spanned 14 films over seven years – as well as some 200 radio broadcasts – and became for generations *the* Holmes-Watson pairing.

The first Rathbone films

Rathbone's first film was the best: a classic rendition of *The Hound of the Baskervilles*, in which Rathbone had second billing to the young lead, Richard Greene, playing Sir Henry Baskerville. It was reasonably faithful to the original and tremendously atmospheric, as Bruce remembered the main set: 'The entire stage was surrounded by a circular screen of canvas on which was painted a very lifelike picture of Dartmoor. The centre of the stage was filled with large boulders made of plaster of Paris. Here and there a bridge was seen and several caves were visible. Running through the boggy, marsh-like ground were several small streams. For eight weeks we worked in this set…' Sharp-eyed viewers of the film will spot the occasional repetitious boulder, but it really was an effective set, and evidence of the (literal) investment in the project by Twentieth Century Fox.

The film, released in 1939, was a critical and popular success; it also had a most surprising – and daring – closing line, as Rathbone's Holmes airily says:' Oh, Watson – the needle!' The film censors for some reason turned a deaf ear to this. A follow-up was immediately called for, and later in the year the same studio made *The Adventures of Sherlock Holmes* – a portmanteau title for a Moriarty-based film in which the arch-criminal is out to steal the Crown Jewels. This, too, was successful, but Twentieth Century Fox then released the series rights, which were taken up by Universal instead.

The Black Dog, Dartmoor

The move to Universal

This studio was to change the format entirely. Their 11 films became essentially B-movie programmers, lasting not much more than an hour each. Economic in style and approach, there were few production values on show, the Watson character was deliberately changed and, crucially, the first three outings were updated propaganda vehicles with explicit anti-Nazi themes.

The Nigel Bruce interpretation of Dr Watson in the Universal films, while endearing, has nothing to do with Conan Doyle's creation. The studio decided to have Bruce play him as a figure of fun, a more-or-less bumbling fool (he was once described as 'Boobus Britannicus' and the epithet has stuck). An American writer, Loren D. Estelman, summed up the Universal characterisation brutally: 'If a mop bucket appeared in a scene, his foot would be inside it, and if by some sardonic twist of fate and the whim of director Roy William Neill he managed to stumble upon an important clue, he could be depended upon to blow his nose on it and throw it away.'

As another writer has justifiably put it: 'Watson was presented as a duffer...who in reality would not have been tolerated by Holmes for five minutes. But that was Bruce's brief. If given a scene as in *Dressed to Kill*...for example, where you have to take a distressed little girl on your knee and make quacking noises like a duck to comfort her, how many ways can you play it?' For anyone yet to see these films, it may come as a surprise to learn that Bruce was actually three years younger than Rathbone.

The first two Universal films, *Sherlock Holmes and the Voice of Terror* and *Sherlock Holmes and the Secret Weapon*, were released in the USA in 1942, by which time the country had entered the war following Pearl Harbour; *Sherlock Holmes in Washington* came out a year later. Holmes quite simply was turned into a Nazi-fighter, and it will not have been purists alone who cringed at the closing words spoken by Holmes in the latter film: '[I]n the days to come the British and American peoples will for their own safety and for the good of all walk together side by side in majesty, in justice and in peace.' Here is Sherlock Holmes directly quoting a speech by Winston Churchill, mentioning the statesman by name. In a sense, of course, it could be taken as a compliment to the stature of the character in popular culture that it was decided to use Holmes in this way. The remaining titles in the Universal series reverted to more or less straightforward mysteries, with *Sherlock Holmes Faces Death* and *Spider Woman* perhaps the best of them.

Rathbone runs away
The Rathbone-Bruce partnership ends

After making *Dressed to Kill* in 1946, Basil Rathbone decided he had had enough. In his 1962 autobiography he recalled how Conan Doyle felt he had to kill Holmes off, and goes on: 'I frankly admit that in 1946 I was placed in a somewhat similar predicament – but *I* could not kill Mr Holmes. So I decided to run away from him. However, to all intents and purposes I might just as well have killed him. My friends excoriated me for my dastardly behaviour, and for a while my long-time friendship with Nigel Bruce suffered severe and recurring shocks. The Music Corporation of America, who represented me at that time, treated me as if I were "sick-sick-sick." '

In 1988 I interviewed Nigel Bruce's daughter Pauline Page, who confirmed her father's sadness at the ending of the partnership: '[T]hey both felt that they had done enough of this – they were their own parts then. But I think that my father was very sad the *way* it was done, which I regret to say was mainly by Basil's wife Ouida, who wanted her husband to go back to playing romantic roles such as in "Romeo and Juliet", which of course he never did because he never really made a success again in a big way after Sherlock Holmes finished. I think it *did* spoil their friendship, it did finish it really, although they did meet again and they had a surface sort of friendship – but a lot of bitterness came into that because they had every opportunity to have gone on.'

BASIL'S BITTERNESS

One quote from Rathbone reaches the heart of his problem with continuing to portray Holmes, and obviously confirms what Pauline Page says (see 'Rathbone runs away'): 'I was… deeply concerned with the problem of being "typed", more completely "typed" than any other classic actor has ever been or ever will be again. My fifty-two roles in twenty-three plays of Shakespeare, my years in the London and New York theatre, my scores of motion pictures, including my two Academy Award

nominations, were slowly but surely sinking into oblivion.' He wrote these self-serving words in 1962, but it is difficult to think of any other leading actor in the intervening years with whom Rathbone's situation can be compared. His last two films were entitled **The Ghost in the Invisible Bikini** *and* **Hillbillys in a Haunted House** *(1966 and 1967).*

Up to date
More Holmes on stage, Part 2

After *The Return of Sherlock Holmes* (see 'Post Gillette's masterpiece') nothing of much interest turned up on the stage until 1953, when two wildly different presentations were mounted. The first was at Sadler's Wells in London, in the form of a ballet called *The Great Detective* (clearly Holmes), with the soon-to-be-famous choreographer Kenneth Macmillan dancing the eponymous rôle. A disaster launched on Broadway in October of the same year, with a play starring no less a personage than Basil Rathbone as Holmes. The show was called, quite simply, *Sherlock*

Jeremy Brett as Holmes and Edward Hardwicke as Watson

Holmes, but had nothing to do with the Gillette original. It was a vanity project, written by Rathbone's wife, and closed after three performances.

Broadway was to embrace Holmes rather more fondly – to the extent, at least, of 313 performances – with a mainstream musical built around the character. It was *Baker Street – The Musical* in 1965, whose book was by Jerome Coopersmith who received a Tony Award nomination for the show and later went on to write for television series such as *Hawaii Five-O*. Two points of interest regarding this: the slender romantic plot was set during Queen Victoria's

Diamond Jubilee year of 1897, and if you look down the cast list you will see the name of Christopher Walken – 13 years before his Oscar-winning performance in *The Deer Hunter*. There was a second musical in 1989, *Sherlock Holmes – The Musical*, which came with the musical credentials of Leslie Bricusse (*Stop The World, I Want To Get Off; Pickwick; Dr Doolittle*) who wrote the book, music and lyrics, and had Ron Moody playing Holmes. The reviews could not even be described as 'mixed' and the production only lasted five weeks in the West End.

The Sherlock Holmes revival of the 1970s and 1980s led to a number of actors trying their hands at Holmes in different ways and in different styles. The Royal Shakespeare Company's revival of Gillette's *Sherlock Holmes* led the way, but Keith Michell and Susan Hampshire had some success in 1979 in the London production of *The Crucifer of Blood*, a version of *The Sign of Four*. Nigel Stock – who had played Dr Watson to the Holmes of both Douglas Wilmer and Peter Cushing on the BBC in the 1960s – toured with a one-man show entitled *221B* in 1983. Rather movingly, he acted Watson reminiscing in Baker Street when he believes Holmes to be lying dead beneath the Reichenbach Falls. The international success of the Granada television series starring Jeremy Brett led to a slightly whimsical stage show by one of the television scriptwriters entitled *The Secret of Sherlock Holmes*, written as a vehicle for Brett and his second Watson, Edward Hardwicke. Basically a sort of dramatic 'greatest hits' play, it ran in London in 1988 and 1989 and has provided employment for actors such as Peter Egan subsequently.

The birth of societies
With their roots firmly in scholarship

Five months before Sir Arthur Conan Doyle's death on 7 July 1930, an article had appeared in the English literary journal *Life & Letters* entitled 'Prolegomena to the Life of Doctor Watson'. It was penned by S. C. Roberts, who we have already seen wrote a review of Ronald Knox's foundation paper 'Studies in the Literature of Sherlock Holmes' (see 'The bright Ronald Knox'). He had now moved on to writing a full biography of Watson.

In October 1932, two major books of what was soon to be called 'Holmesian' (in Britain) or 'Sherlockian' (in the USA) scholarship appeared. T. S. Blakeney produced a volume whose verbose title summed up the game immediately: *Sherlock Holmes: Fact or Fiction? – The First Really Authoritative Biography of this Famous Detective*. And H. W. Bell published *Sherlock Holmes & Doctor Watson – A Chronology of their Adventures*. Bell was especially pleased to receive a letter of congratulation

ENGLISH HERITAGE

DOROTHY L. SAYERS
1893-1957
Writer of
Detective Stories
lived here
1921-1929

from the crime writer Dorothy L. Sayers, who had created the character Lord Peter Wimsey over a decade earlier; she then engaged in a detailed correspondence with him regarding the date involved in 'The Red-Headed League'.

The first society

Bell was already considering editing a collection of papers on Sherlock Holmes and invited Sayers to become one of the contributors. She agreed to do so, as did Ronald Knox, S. C. Roberts, the Chicago-based American newspaper man Vincent Starrett and the satirical writer A. G. Macdonell (author of *England Their England*). The volume, entitled *Baker Street Studies*, appeared in 1934 and with it, the nucleus of what was to become the first British Sherlock Holmes Society; others joined via the Detection Club, which Sayers had co-founded in 1928.

In April 1934, Macdonell invited some enthusiasts to a sherry party (how English!) and Roberts later reported that 'those present declared themselves to be the Sherlock Holmes Society'. Inevitably a dinner followed on 6 June, held at a long-disappeared restaurant, Canuto's in Baker Street. However the Society, such as it then was, really only existed for two more annual dinners and never instigated any publications; it was dissolved in March 1938. It was another 13 years before a second Society was founded – which exists to this day and celebrated its own Diamond Jubilee in 2011.

The Baker Street Irregulars

Meanwhile, at the same time in the USA, Vincent Starrett, who had penned a Sherlock Holmes pastiche back in 1920, was hot on Holmes' tracks, having written what was to become another early cornerstone collection of essays, *The Private Life of Sherlock Holmes*, published in 1933. Furthermore, the essayist, journalist and novelist Christopher Morley was giving regular mention to Sherlock Holmes matters in his column in *The Saturday Review of Literature*; indeed he and his three brothers back in 1902 had dubbed themselves 'The Sign of the Four'. Morley also liked lunches, long, gossipy, literary lunches – and in 1930 had been asked to write a Preface to a new two-volume edition of the whole run of Sherlock Holmes stories. Everything was in place for the founding of another Society.

Drinks were held in January 1934 and a tongue-in-cheek Constitution published the following month: the purpose of the society was 'the study of the Sacred Writings…All other business shall be left for the monthly meeting. There shall be no monthly meeting.' The first dinner was held at a restaurant in New York on 7 December. Among those present were Morley, Starrett, the former World Heavyweight Boxing Champion, Gene Tunney, and two other men famous in the field of Sherlock

Holmes: William Gillette and the illustrator Frederic Dorr Steele. They called themselves the Baker Street Irregulars. The Irregular Constitution also carried the words 'All persons shall be eligible for membership who pass an examination in the Sacred Writings'; but that line carried with it an assumption. Amazingly, women could not become full members until 1991. The Irregulars started publishing a quarterly journal in 1946, *The Baker Street Journal*.

The Sherlock Holmes Society of London

In 1950, preparations were being made for the following year's Festival of Britain – an attempt to lift the country out of post-Second World War blues. All sorts of events were mounted by local councils and London boroughs – and the borough of St Marylebone was not to be left out. Their councillors had a bright idea: they would stage an exhibition about changes to the area over the previous century, especially highlighting slum clearance. Utterly worthy – and utterly dull – was the general consensus.

Another idea had been put forward: that the borough should mount an exhibition about one of its most famous residents, a certain Sherlock Holmes. This was not found acceptable, and press coverage of a most extraordinary nature ensued, specifically in the letters column of *The Times*. Missives were published from, among others, Dr Watson, Mycroft Holmes and Mrs Hudson, not to mention the famous film actor Arthur Wontner. All of these letters argued, of course, how wrong the councillors were and how the idea of a Holmes exhibition must proceed. Indeed *The Times* carried a leader on the matter, as did the *New York Herald Tribune*.

The inevitable happened, and on 22 May 1951 a Sherlock Holmes Exhibition was opened at Abbey House, a building in Baker Street, north of the Marylebone Road, whose address covered No. 221. The four enthusiasts who put the exhibition together had another bright idea: to reform the long-defunct Sherlock Holmes Society. They added the words 'of London' and it is by that name that the

Society still exists. The inaugural meeting was held on 17 July 1951 at the Victoria and Albert Museum. Installed as President was the long-time scholarly enthusiast S. C. Roberts, by now Master of Pembroke College, Cambridge.

The Society's first chairman was R. Ivar Gunn – who by an extraordinary coincidence had been at New College, Oxford, in 1911 together with Christopher Morley (over from the USA as a Rhodes Scholar) and in the same year as Ronald Knox had first read his seminal paper on Sherlock Holmes in that very university. Others present at the first meeting included Paul Gore-Booth – later the head of Britain's Home Civil Service – and Winifred Paget, daughter of the great *Strand Magazine* Holmes illustrator. The following year, the Society launched its own publication, *The Sherlock Holmes Journal,* which is still published twice a year; its first editor was one James Edward Holroyd – the person who initially suggested that Marylebone should put on an Exhibition devoted to Sherlock Holmes.

An insatiable appetite
Holmes and modern media

While the ever-increasing number of Sherlock Holmes 'scholars' joined societies around the world – and had fun writing about Watson's wives and Holmes' university – radio, television and cinema developed an insatiable appetite for the character.

Radio

NBC was the first broadcaster to put Holmes on the wireless, with William Gillette starring in 'The Speckled Band' in October 1930. He was only there for that first show; an actor named Richard Gordon played the lead role in most of the near 200 subsequent series broadcasts that continued up to 1936. Two years later, Orson Welles and his Mercury Theatre of the Air presented an atmospheric version of the Gillette play. Then in 1939, Basil Rathbone and Nigel Bruce embarked upon an amazing run of 218 radio dramatisations. Rathbone pulled out of playing the character in 1946, but Bruce's Watson appeared in a further season of 39 weekly half-hours. As with the Gordon series, this series was an extended amalgam of original stories and new ones with titles like 'The Dentist who used Wolfbane', 'The Haunted Bagpipes' and 'Murder by Remote Control'.

In 1943, BBC radio began to show an interest, and produced a fascinating one-off broadcast in July that year of 'The Boscombe Valley Mystery' – fascinating because while it was perfectly feasible to cast Arthur Wontner as Holmes, Watson was played by Carleton Hobbs. In brief, Hobbs was later cast in the leading rôle and played Holmes off and on from 1952 until 1969. His Dr Watson was to be Norman Shelley, who had been a huge hit on the radio programme 'Children's Hour' as Winnie the Pooh.

A major radio highlight took place on the evening of 21 December 1954 when, at the end of an entirely different BBC-produced series, one of the finest cast Sherlock Holmes dramatisations was broadcast. 'The Final Problem' starred John Gielgud and Ralph Richardson as Holmes and Watson respectively – and Orson

Orson Welles

Welles as Professor Moriarty.

Triumphantly, on 5 July 1998, BBC radio was able to celebrate something no other broadcasting organisation had ever even attempted: the completion of a full series of the 60 stories, with the same two actors – Clive Merrison and Michael Williams – playing the main two rôles throughout. On one occasion, when the actress playing the housekeeper Mrs Hudson was ill, the director of the episode smuggled someone else into BBC Broadcasting House to deliver the words that needed to be spoken. It happened to be Williams's wife, Judi Dench.

Television

Television has been hugely influential on the Sherlock Holmes boom, but began very late. There was an early six-show series on the BBC in the autumn of 1951; yet importantly, an actor who looked the part of Sherlock Holmes perfectly was cast in the rôle for what might have been a one-off appearance, in 'The Speckled Band'. Douglas Wilmer – a successful supporting star in films such as Laurence Olivier's *Richard III* and *El Cid,* as Charlton Heston's sidekick – was teamed with a stalwart stage and film actor, Nigel Stock, and fortuitously the pair ended up making a total of 13 episodes from 1964 to 1965. Wilmer was both a stickler for accuracy and an actor who knew what effort was required by a team to make a successful show; the show was successful, but the actor left, leaving Peter Cushing to take up the torch in 1968 instead.

If Wilmer was the Holmes for the 1960s, there's no doubt who satiated the continued desire for the character on television in the 1980s and 1990s. Granada cast the flamboyant actor Jeremy Brett in the rôle; he embraced the part while explaining to interviewers that he would not have crossed the road to meet Sherlock Holmes. Initially, there was money available and fine production values were met as Brett hit the screens in 1984, at first with David Burke as his Watson and thereafter with Edward Hardwicke. Yet over the next decade he appeared in 41 episodes, which deteriorated in quality as the television company began to rate the brand above what had hitherto been superior production; Brett's health also became an issue. While Wilmer and Cushing had played their rôles in line with what they believed was the viewing public's idea of Holmes, Brett – at least in the early episodes – chose an exciting, excitable, occasionally hyper-active, and always affected, portrayal. There was self-preening and an occasional outburst of over-the-top nostril flaring in his portrayal of Holmes; nevertheless he became a worldwide success. His final appearance was in 1994 – and it would be 17 years before the next, extraordinary, television appearance of Holmes (see 'Enduring appeal').

Cinema

After Rathbone and Bruce finished on the screen in the mid-1940s, major Sherlock Holmes films were irregular. Peter Cushing gave *The Hound of the Baskervilles* a Hammer (Horror) Films treatment in 1959. Six years later, the classically-trained John Neville played a very believable Holmes in a lurid Jack the Ripper movie, *A Study in Terror*; such films always attracted good quality casts and this one was no exception, starring Anthony Quayle, Barbara Windsor, Frank Finlay and a young Judi Dench.

No further film of any substance, bar one, *The Private Life of Sherlock Holmes*, came until 1978 – and then it was another version of the Ripper story. This time it starred Christopher Plummer as Holmes, maintaining cast quality with an appearance by Sir John Gielgud as the Prime Minister, and no less than James Mason as Watson. Anything to do with

Christopher Plummer

Sherlock Holmes, amazingly, still had, in media terms, audience potential. And, as with television, the wider screen was to take a daring chance to reinvent, but not until 2009 (see 'Enduring appeal').

THE PRIVATE LIFE OF SHERLOCK HOLMES

There are film directors, and there are great film directors. It is an extraordinary example of the attraction of the Sherlock Holmes character and what may be done with it that one of the very greatest directors directed a Holmes film. It was a critical success and popular failure at the time, but has become the cult Holmes film. **The Private Life of Sherlock Holmes** *(1970)* was the product of a long Holmesian gestation period from Billy Wilder *(***Some Like It Hot, Sunset Boulevard, The Apartment** and *all his other great films). He brought the Shakespearean-trained actors* **Robert Stephens** *and* **Colin Blakely** *to the Holmes and Watson rôles, and then threw in some adventure and a love interest. The film studio called for massive cuts to protect their investment and the end product – interesting as it is – is not what Wilder set out to achieve.*

Enduring appeal
Holmes in the 21st century

The first story, *A Study in Scarlet*, appeared in 1887; the last Holmes story by Conan Doyle was published 40 years later. Parodies, pastiches, plays, films, radio and television series, as well as every other form of media exposure, have kept Sherlock Holmes at the very front line of brand usage for more than 120 years. It is an amazing feat and one which the creator would never have believed possible – and certainly would never have embraced. Even people like Christopher Morley and Vincent Starrett in 1930s USA (this is the moment to reveal that Franklin Roosevelt was a Baker Street Irregular) – or Dorothy L. Sayers and Paul Gore-Booth in Britain (and this is the moment to reveal that Agatha Christie was a guest of honour at a Sherlock Holmes Society Annual Dinner) would not have predicted the longevity of the public's love affair with Holmes.

Yet in 2009, film director Guy Ritchie achieved worldwide acclaim with *Sherlock Holmes* – an extravaganza of a film starring A-list actors Robert Downie Jr and Jude Law, which seemed initially to have nothing to do with the original characters other than their names. Yet the film, despite its computer-game elements and action antics, retained that paramount Holmes-Watson bond – built on dry humour and true companionship, whatever missile is hurtling towards them. This huge success was followed in 2012 by *Sherlock Holmes: A Game of Shadows*, a film that this time aimed successfully to adhere, however extravagantly, to a Conan Doyle story, 'The Final Problem'. A purist would say that these two films are modern action movies, which merely involve Holmes and Watson in outsize form. A realist would say that they are a clever way to keep the basic format alive in a manner that echoes the original, while reinventing for modern audiences.

Exactly the same can be said for the television sensation *Sherlock*, starring Benedict Cumberbatch and Martin Freeman. Writers Stephen Moffat and Mark Gatiss thought that Sherlock Holmes should be brought

Benedict Cumberbatch
as Holmes

into the 21st century, but that vital nods of appreciation to the original should be given in each 90-minute episode. Thus, for example, viewers around the world have seen versions of *The Hound of the Baskervilles* and 'A Scandal in Bohemia' that are cleverly transposed to a modern time, yet utterly faithful – and with constantly subtle allusions to Conan Doyle's

conceptions. Awards for the writers and actors abound. And there have been female fans of the series that have decreed that they should be named 'Cumberbitches'.

There may never have been 'Paget-page turners', 'Gillette-adorers' or 'Wilmer-worshippers' in quite the same way, but it is a mark of the enduring appeal of this – let us not forget it – fictional character that every generation of Holmes fan has invented new ways of enjoying Conan Doyle's creation.

Epilogue
Remembering Conan Doyle

In 1974, the publishers John Murray released a new complete edition of all the Sherlock Holmes stories. To lend the event some punch, special introductions to each volume were commissioned. The list of names of those who agreed to contribute was truly distinguished: Grahame Greene, C. P. Snow, Kingsley Amis, John Fowles, Angus Wilson, Hugh Greene, Eric Ambler, Len Deighton and Julian Symons.

It is just possible that something Arthur Conan Doyle wrote in 1912 had struck a chord with these leading writers. It was not in a Sherlock Holmes story, but four simple lines of verse he penned for the opening of his Professor Challenger tale, *The Lost World*:

Eric Ambler

'I have wrought my simple plan
If I give one hour of joy
To the boy who's half a man,
Or the man who's half a boy'

More directly relevant, perhaps, are the words of a poem entitled '221B' and written by the American Sherlock Holmes enthusiast Vincent Starrett. There has never been a better summing-up:

'Here dwell together still two men of note
Who never lived and so can never die:
How very near they seem, yet how remote
That age before the world went all awry.
But still the game's afoot for those with ears
Attuned to catch the distant view-halloo:
England is England yet, for all our fears –
Only those things the heart believes are true.
A yellow fog swirls past the window-pane
As night descends upon this fabled street:
A lonely hansom splashes through the rain,
The ghostly gas lamps fail at twenty feet.
Here, though the world explode, these two survive,
And it is always 1895.'

BIBLIOGRAPHY

Conan Doyle, A. *Memories and Adventures,* Hodder & Stoughton, 1924

Dudley Edwards, O. (Ed.) *The Oxford Sherlock Holmes*, Oxford University Press, 1993

Lancelyn Green, R. and Gibson, J.M. *A Bibliography of A. Conan Doyle,* The Clarendon Press, Oxford, 1983

Lellenberg, J., Stashower, D. and Foley, C. (Eds.) *Arthur Conan Doyle – A Life in Letters*, HarperPress, 2007

Lycett, A. *Conan Doyle – The Man who created Sherlock Holmes,* Weidenfeld & Nicolson, 2007

Pointer, M. *The Public Life of Sherlock Holmes,* David & Charles, 1975

Rathbone, B. *In and Out of Character – An Autobiography*, Doubleday & Co. 1962

The Sherlock Holmes Journal, The Sherlock Holmes Society of London, 1952 –

The Strand Magazine, George Newnes Ltd, 1891 – 1950

Tracy, J. *The Encyclopaedia Sherlockiana,* Jack Doubleday & Co, 1977

Utechin, N. *From Piff-Pouff to Backnecke – Ronald Knox and 100 Years of "Studies in the Literature of Sherlock Holmes"*, The Baker Street Irregulars, 2010

Utechin, N. *'A Golden Day' – Arthur Conan Doyle at the Langham Hotel, Friday 30th August 1889,* The Sherlock Holmes Society of London, 2010

Warrack, G. *Sherlock Holmes and Music*, Faber & Faber, 1947

Zecher, H. *William Gillette, America's Sherlock Holmes,* Xlibris, USA, 2011

INDEX

PICTURE CREDITS

Page 48 © http://www.221b.ch/index_e.html

Page 126 © *Carl Van Vechten estate*

These files are licensed under the Creative Commons Attribution-Share Alike 3.0 Unported license.

Page 9 © BotMultichill at en.wikipedia

Page 28 © Author ΛΦΠ

Page 31 © Langhamhotelsinternational

Page 36 © Photograph by MichaelMaggs; original artist unknown.

These files are licensed under the Creative Commons Attribution 2.0 Generic license.

Page 25 © gailf548

Page 42 © Andrew Dunn, 19 September 2004. Website: http://www.andrewdunnphoto.com

Page 46 © Freedom Fry – «Happy birthday to GNU» film crew, especially Matt Lee and Andrew Sampson, derivative work: Beao

Page 50 © Wikid77 at en.wikipedia. File Upload Bot (Magnus Manske)

Page 76 © Author Michael Yew

Page 87 © Herbythyme

Page 111 © Author unknown, Deutsches Bundesarchiv (German Federal Archive)

Page 122 © Mike Quinn

Page 128 © Courtney. Diaa abdelmoneim

Page 129 © Alan Light

Page 131 © Fat Les, derivative work: RanZag (talk).

MORE AMAZING TITLES

LOVED THIS BOOK?

Tell us what you think and you could win another fantastic book from David & Charles in our monthly prize draw.

www.lovethisbook.co.uk

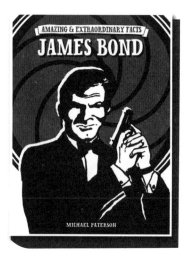

AMAZING & EXTRAORDINARY FACTS: JAMES BOND
Michael Paterson
ISBN: 978-1-4463-0195-1

The essential companion for every Bond fan, unearthing a selection of surprising and intruiging facts about the much-loved fictional spy, and the books and films that he has starred in. It is brimming with strange and amusing stories about the Bond actors, from Sean Connery to Daniel Craig, behind the scenes at the film set, and amazing facts about Ian Fleming's original novels.

AMAZING & EXTRAORDINARY FACTS: LONDON
Stephen Halliday
ISBN: 978-0-7153-3910-7

A unique collection of strange laws, heroic deeds, surprising revelations and other quirky stories that have shaped the unique history of Britain's capital. London's long history is an extraordinarily rich source of amazing facts, whether your interest is political, social, architectural or historical, you will find a variety of topics in this alternative guide to London.

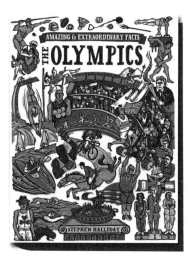

AMAZING & EXTRAORDINARY FACTS: THE OLYMPICS
Stephen Halliday
ISBN: 978-1-4463-0201-9

A unique and entertaining collection of facts surrounding the Olympic Games. From their origins in ancient Greece to the most famous Olympic medalists, the book covers a range of fascinating trivia for every sport lover to enjoy. You can discover the athletes who have set the marks for modern sporting excellence, and wonder at the records set by competitors across the years.

A DAVID & CHARLES BOOK
© F&W Media International, Ltd 2012

David & Charles is an imprint of F&W Media International, Ltd
Brunel House, Forde Close, Newton Abbot, TQ12 4PU, UK

F&W Media International, Ltd is a subsidiary of F+W Media, Inc
10151 Carver Road, Suite #200, Blue Ash, OH 45242, USA

Text and Designs © Nicholas Utechin 2012
Layout © F&W Media International, Ltd 2012

First published in the UK and USA in 2012

A catalogue record for this book is available from the British Library.

ISBN-13: 978-1-4463-0268-2 hardback
ISBN-10: 1-4463-0268-7 hardback

Printed in China by Toppan Leefung Printing Limited for:
F&W Media International, Ltd
Brunel House, Forde Close, Newton Abbot, TQ12 4PU, UK

10 9 8 7 6 5 4 3 2 1

Junior Acquisitions Editor: Verity Graves-Morris
Assistant Editor: Hannah Kelly
Project Editor: Freya Dangerfield
Junior Designer: Jennifer Stanley
Production Manager: Beverley Richardson

F+W Media publishes high quality books on a wide range of subjects.
For more great book ideas visit: www.fwmedia.co.uk